UP FROM PARALYSIS

a true story

Joseph Seiler

BALBOA
PRESS
A DIVISION OF HAY HOUSE

Balboa Press books may be ordered through booksellers or by contacting:

Balboa Press
A Division of Hay House
1663 Liberty Drive
Bloomington, IN 47403
www.balboapress.com
1-(877) 407-4847

Printed in the United States of America.

Name of Editor; Nancy Roberts, Dartmouth Nova Scotia

ISBN: 978-1-4525-7478-3 (sc)
ISBN: 978-1-4525-7480-6 (hc)
ISBN: 978-1-4525-7479-0 (e)

Library of Congress Control Number: 2013909466

Balboa Press rev. date: 6/5/2013

TABLE OF CONTENTS

Dedicated to
Barb
My life partner
Who endured and stayed
Even though as helpless as I
To do anything about it

Thank you, dear Barb

FOREWORD

Joseph has been a friend for close to twenty years now. It was our professional careers that first brought us together. Here we were, two electrical engineers collaborating on a project to be the first in the world to use satellite technology for reading utility meters. We thought we were on the precipice of technology. Yet, looking back, neither of us owned a cell phone, let alone would have predicted the unbelievable functionality that exists in them today.

Joe and I "clicked." And since the early '90s we have gone overnight wilderness camping together, run together in the blistering heat and the freezing cold. We attended the same church, my wife and I attended the Seiler's amazing themed charity dinner parties and for three years, Joe was my coach. During this time we talked for fifteen minutes to an hour every single week.

From all of these adventures, there is one thing about Joseph Seiler for which I am most grateful – he made me look at myself differently and look at my role in the world differently. Thank you for that, Joe. And thank you for not forcing this self-reflection upon me. Thank you for your gentle nudges instead, disguised as insightful questions.

In *Up From Paralysis,* Joe shares a very personal experience that has deeply touched him. He has taken this experience and invited us to join in his journey … to seek and to wonder what it all means. You will never hear him telling you what you should do or think, but you'll feel some gentle nudges.

Joe's unique perspective on the world is empowering. He offers some thoughts and insights, and in his true humble fashion would not think that what he has learned would absolutely apply to you or to me. Further, he confesses that he has much to learn and does not purport to have it all figured out.

I respect his humility, but frankly, this book does have something for you.

You will see the world differently after sharing in Joe's journey. I am not sure what you will take away from his surreal GBS experience but you cannot read this story and be unchanged.

You might find rekindled hope or pick up a neat trick to help you sleep instead of tossing and turning. Joe is a master at noticing what is invisible to others and then revealing it to them. He does not disappoint. <u>Watch him as you read</u>.

I know the next time I pick up this book I will find something totally new in the pages … as if it had not been there when I read it last. As you read, take from Joe's experience what is there for you and enjoy getting to know yourself better through the experiences of this courageous man and wonderful human being (and enjoy getting to know Joseph).

Steve Foran
The Gratitude Guy
Halifax, Nova Scotia
www.steveforan.com

UP FROM PARALYSIS

INTRODUCTION

The probability of experiencing the disease GBS, twice in a lifetime, is less than 1 in 1,000,000. It happened to me.

I became severely paralyzed and my mind became ultra aware of receiving messages in the form of dreams and words and felt sense, from what I believe is the Divine speaking directly to me. The two events of paralysis occurred over a period of 13 years, during which I continued to gain clarity in the interpretation of those messages. The second instance of GBS occurred in 2013 and it greatly enhanced and solidified my understanding. The paramount message is that there is a way to communicate, receive Guidance, from a Source greater than human, that is available to all. My experience of learning about this is shared in these pages.

I have come up from paralysis in both the physical sense and in my clarity about what Divine is and how It works. I am no guru, but rather a fellow human being who had an extraordinary experience that increased my clarity and my happiness in life.

One of the messages to me was that I write this book to share my discoveries with you.

Up From Paralysis is about **getting really clear** about what I am (you are).

About getting really clear about what I (you) want.

About getting ever more clear about how to go and get what I (you) want.

About **living my (your) life viewed through the lens of clarity** gained through the Guidance available to us all.

And about the GBS journeys wherein I twice experienced paralysis and recovery, in a strangely joyful way.

MY BEGINNINGS

I was born of immigrant parents and spoke other than English for the first five years of my life. My father passed when I was only thirteen years old. We lived on welfare and the kind assistance of others until I left home to join the Navy as an ROTP graduate in engineering. Until then I had little understanding or regard or time for things spiritual. I mowed lawns, shoveled snow, delivered flyers and shared a paper route in order to keep up with friends who got an allowance of a massive $5 every week. I started smoking at age eleven and had been to juvenile court three times by the time I was fifteen, plus, once spent a few nights in a juvenile detention center (that was a game-changing bad place and I am grateful now that I was sent there).

My school marks were generally excellent. School was easy, almost boring at times. I had a lot of spare capacity to use for getting myself into trouble. I finally changed and became a better contributor to the family. I was the oldest of four and my European Mom really was not comfortable without "a man" around to do the man stuff, though she was one tough person, a real she-bear, when it came to going to bat for her children.

Once married, Barb and I moved to the other end of the country and began parenting three beautiful girls (Carmen, Cathy, Leslie) in our new home together. I became curious about all this religion stuff at age twenty-six. Actually, I became quite inconvenienced that I had to strip out of my coveralls, get washed up and go to church in the middle of my enjoyments working on cars. Yet, as a logical type and somewhat practical, even if not always careful, I decided that I ought to check out this God thing, just in case there was something to it. I was having this thought walking down the road on a bright clear day and formed the idea of asking for "a sign." A drop of water landed squarely on my head. No, not a bird, I wiped it and smelled it. It was water. No overhead wires or tree branches, no source for this large water droplet. Wow, ask for a sign, boom, sign delivered. What was this?

I then volunteered to teach the Confirmation class, ninth-grade young adults around fourteen years old, at our church. I chose that group because that particular class was almost obligatory, at least according to the parents, and, the participants were mature enough to actually think about things, if I could challenge and invite them in the right way. I liked that idea. I didn't know what I had signed up for.

Suddenly I was reading constantly and asking a lot of questions myself. There was a pastor from a different church living across the street. I asked him for help and he lent me two volumes by Barclay (a historian specializing in interpreting scripture) that review the Gospel According to Matthew. I also read *An Historian's Review of the Gospels* by Grant. Well, talk about being released from the tyranny of the pulpit. These books showed me that it is within each person that the idea and the relationship with God is formed and nurtured and grown. I came to know that there is indeed a God and that He/She is more than friendly. She/He is Love and, beyond that, **is only Love**.

For a left-brained, male, military engineer this was a massive change in perspective.

The main stream of this book is written around my stint with Guillain-Barre Syndrome (GBS), one of the MS family of diseases, which I encountered near my fiftieth birthday. So many insights came together, became clear, around that time. Though my body was unable to do much of anything, my mind was unaffected by the disease. In fact, I found that my mind was hyper-alert, as if on steroids. I had a lot of time to just think using that super-aware mind.

Up From Paralysis shares the learning I have found, not just at the time of the disease but in the thirteen years since. I have been privileged to have come up from paralysis to a rare clarity, rare for me, about what Divine is, how to interact with It and why that has been a good thing to do. I want to share this with you and anyone else who might be interested.

My website still has the original story of my sojourn in year 2000.

tinyurl.com/am2aj8w

The website version has been very slightly edited to make things clearer for use in this book.

Having offered the disclaimer in the opening lines of this book, I can also say that the knowing that I am to share has been known for a long time.

The Universe is not outside of you.
Look inside yourself;
Everything that you want,
You already are.

Rumi

Rumi lived centuries ago and he has just given us the greatest piece of wisdom that exists. Einstein said similar things and many a sage has tried to show our species the way. For some reason, we won't listen. I think it is all about the persona of our ego that is yakking away in our minds 24/7. It is trying to convince us we are in grave danger and must and should and can't and never and always and just any angle on a fearsome existence that it can invent. It is a very inventive persona and can be quite convincing. Let us see what we can find by keeping that persona on notice. It won't stop yakking, but we can stop listening.

A very short guide to the code of this book:

- There are three different font styles from this point onward. This type, which you are reading now, is used when writing about the course of the two GBS experiences in 2000 and 2013. These are the chronicles of my GBS disease, the hospital time and related events. I wrote a brief story about the year 2000 GBS, which included insights from that time. Those are also in this same font

- There are many paragraphs in this second font style, that you are reading now, covering my present insights and discoveries in reflecting about the GBS in 2000 and about the 13 years since then, plus, after GBS2 which happened in January 2013. So this second font type is primarily reflection and discovery, all written in Spring 2013.

- A number of emails are included, verbatim, in their own typeface as taken from the computer that sent and received them. That means there are three different font types to help you to understand when something was written and for what purpose.

MY FIRST DAYS WITH GBS

It seemed an ordinary Tuesday (March 29, 2000), a gentle three-mile run before breakfast and my usual one morning a week of consulting support to SEIMAC, the company I sold to three employee colleagues nearly two years ago. It was raining and I didn't much enjoy wearing my rain gear because the end of March is still rather cold on the motorcycle. I decided not to wear my gloves and get them soaked while I made a handful of deliveries on my way home. The temperature was just cold enough that my hands became stiff as I rode from place to place. By the time I got home my left hand was feeling particularly stiff, from using the clutch I had surmised, but somehow it was more than that. I wasn't quite sure I should engage the clutch one more time to put the Harley into the garage. But I managed.

Something was not right.

Barb had opened wine for dinner and as I warmed up all seemed fine. But when I raised my left hand with the wine glass I nearly dropped it as I passed shoulder height. Hmmmm? What is this?

I went to bed early and noticed a slight tingling at the end of the center three fingers of my right hand. It would leave me by morning, I thought, as would the hint of a flu that seemed to have been in my throat the past few days. I am not one to be sick.

I knew something was up when I tried next morning and failed, to put on my sock, thinking I would go to the gym, as usual. "Barb, I think we have a problem." My left leg failed me in going out the front door and down the two steps to the driveway. I was flat on my back faster than I can remember. I wept. I was afraid.

Denial is the first reaction to "something" happening to me, like losing a whack on the stock market. I was in denial that my attention was being sought, big time.

My thoughts after falling down those steps continued along the lines of "this can't be happening to me." I like to understand and I could make no sense of this. Denial.

The insistence on having a logical trail to everything is one of our downfalls as a species. It keeps us from much happiness. What would be wrong with someone helping me, a person I have not yet met, helping me to carry something from my car, for instance? Must there be a logical reason for this act of kindness? Well, if I am female and this helper is a male, what thoughts could that ego of mine come up with? A simple situation and a possible happy or a possible unhappy feeling, depending on which way my thinking goes. If I do not "notice" my thinking much I could find myself in with a lot of negative and fearful thoughts as I go about my day. What if I didn't get any help with the package and many people just walked by? Let the ego do the thinking unchecked and a string of not-so-happy can come rolling out.

There is more to this. As I think, I then act. So if I decide that the world is against me and the observation that no one volunteered to help me is put into the pot, imagine where the thinking could go. Keep that scenario going and let my day unfold. Let people need help from me. How am I likely to respond with this "world is against me" idea becoming ever more fully established in my mind? That "voice" we all have in our heads could be having a pity-fest and my willingness to engage and contribute to my world could be shrinking.

Our human condition includes that voice. We all have it. If I pay attention to what it is saying, I can then take a thought or leave it. If I do not pay attention, the voice rolls and I believe what it tells me. Results can go away from happiness and I might not even notice until I am low enough to be seeking medication or professional help. Sound extreme? I believe we have all had a bout of down-spiral thinking where we are worn out at the end of the day because that negative fearful yak-yak will not stop tearing me down.

Until I notice it, I am in the tentacles of my fear-filled internal voice. Lesson one.

The doctor was afraid too when there was no reflex response from tapping my knee or my elbow. He phoned the hospital, prepared a hurried note for the emergency staff and sent me off doing his best not to show his anxiousness.

The doc was in denial too, accompanied by a rising amount of sweat on his forehead. Was I dying? Was this an exit scene? It wasn't painful in a physical way but it was oh so unknown and separate from my understanding. I don't exactly recall my thinking on the way to the hospital. It was a kind of surreal trip. I was sort of detached from the world, feeling very alone and without control of anything. This brought forth more denial-type thinking and I had a list of possible trivial reasons all of this was happening. Pinched nerve, something blocked, imbalanced inner ear stuff. I was reaching but still had not hit stage two, anger. Denial was still king.

It took three guys to get me out of the car at the emergency because I was unable to use my legs. A hundred questions asked a hundred times, over and over. It was thought that I may have Guillain-Barre Syndrome and by suppertime I was scheduled to go to the intensive care unit because they "wanted to monitor my breathing."

I had not yet been told that it was GBS. Why not? Was it too scary a disease to mention as a possibility? Or was this their denial of the increasingly obvious?

We humans are not that good at listening to our intuition, our Spirit, our Guides, our inner wisdom. For the most part we treat our body as a dumb object, somehow almost inanimate, with only our brain telling it everything to do – pump the blood, breathe the lungs, wash the car, heal that cut, buy some eggs, etc. Not many notice that the body is an amazing antenna to detect "disturbances in the Force" way before the mind detects them. In fact, the mind does not do the detection of anything like that, but only interprets the signals picked up by the body (body as antenna). We hear the phrase, "he is totally in his head" to mean awareness of the rest of the world is so low that response to it is all but zero. We have that wonderful word, "solipsism," to capture this state. Solipsism is the conclusion that the world and other minds do not exist inside one's own mind's interpretation of the world, that therefore nothing besides my own thinking has any meaning.

It took until nearly 4 p.m. for me to admit that I was not going to make it to the client site the next day to facilitate a workshop. Denial was starting to weaken. Yet my thought was that the workshop would be rescheduled to next week or so. I could not bear any thought of a longer delay, meaning a longer hospital stay… or worse.

I had just worked my very last day at my company, now sold to three employee colleagues. A chapter had ended on that day in March. My ego had just been disconnected from that which had defined much of its worth for many years. Part of me had dissolved and no longer existed. This was change on steroids, bigger than big. Though bravely putting on a face of Acceptance, deep inside this little voice wondered how soon I'd be forgotten. Sheesh, what a thought. In such a state, which I did not realize I was in at the time, is it any wonder that my body resistance was down? I was vulnerable to any drive by germ or virus and boom, GBS. But why this particular invasion of my body?

"Something we were withholding made us weak. Until we found out that it was ourselves" —Robert Frost

What might I have been withholding? I now vote for acknowledgment that I was quite comfortable in my role as the owner and leader of that company. We were successful and the company was me. I knew what to do and could do it repeatedly. I was about to step off a cliff into an unknown. I was comfortable looking back and in denial about looking forward.

It reminds me of the story where someone falls in a mountain climbing accident. They are hanging by a rope. It is dark. They pray. An answer comes, telling them to cut the rope. Ridiculous answer, huh, cut the rope? No way. In the morning the climber is found frozen to death hanging from a rope less than a foot from the ground. I was not even at the prayer part, let alone the answer part. No wonder I was rudderless and didn't even know that about myself. Denial city.

It was Thursday, March 30. I had only slight movement in my toes and could still move my head. My voice was gone. My breathing was being done by a machine through a tube into my lungs. I was paralyzed from the chin down and lost. The doctor had said the night before, "If we put a tube into you to help you breathe, you will be here for at least four months, ready yourself." I told him I would not stay in the hospital for that long and would see him on the street within a month. It was my first argument with the medical staff, and I was not apologetic over it.

DRUG-INDUCED COMA

The Emerg doctor was the last person to hear my final efforts to speak. In faint rasps I told him I was not staying four or five months. If I could have lifted my finger, he'd have got that too. They had filled me with morphine because I did not want that breathing tube put into me. My fight response was in great form, yet my ability to actually do anything was so near zero that, with the drugs added to the mix, I passed out.

Whom or What was I arguing with? No pain to speak of, just a drifting down to involuntary physical stillness and now the mental journey to "somewhere else" to be given images that I called dreams. These dreams were extraordinarily vivid in their depth of color and sharpness. Very, very IMAX 3D. I was "out" for about three days and had some particularly clear dreams in this stunning Technicolor surround sound format.

Barb had somehow held it together, at least in front of me. I learned later that she was doing her crying in the car on the way to and from the hospital so that she could be strong while with me and the girls. What a woman.

Leslie wasn't told until it was absolutely clear that this was going to last a while, as she was in the midst of her final production and needed to perform in a significant role in the fourth-year university play as part of her drama degree.

By Thursday afternoon it was time to get past denial. Leslie looked at me as I lay paralyzed and said "This one is for you Dad," as she went off to do her duty, as I indeed wanted her to do. Her voice was thick. She collapsed as she entered the preparation room and saw her friends. Her troupe conducted an energy healing circle for me the next evening. I certainly needed it.

That was also the day the priest came. Oh boy, did I freak. He offered to give me the sacrament of the sick. Well for an old Baltimore Catechism Catholic that meant I was about to die. My father had died within hours of receiving the same sacrament, which was then called Extreme Unction and was only given if death was a very real possibility. My father had died when he was fifty. My fiftieth birthday was only a few days away. It took me a minute to update myself about the new spin on that sacrament (for any who are sick). I stopped holding my breath and accepted his offer to give me this sacrament of healing. But I was angry.

Ahh, there we have it, anger. Denial, the first phase toward Acceptance, was finally ending.

Speaking my inside thought was not an available option. So I "endured" the sacrament of healing from the well-intentioned priest. I felt violated. I started to have my dreams. What is it about dreams? I had not given them much importance, but these, they were so vivid and they came more than once. Was I being "spoken to"? That is what it felt like. I was receiving information and maybe even guidance from a Source that knew the future. These dreams were delivered to me from the "other side." One thing was very consistent, I was not a happy camper and resisted it all. I resisted the reality of the situation, the ideas that went with it (long time in hospital) and the inability to move. Two days ago I went for a run! What was this! Anger came. Progress at last.

And the word went out. Joe is very ill. He has GBS. The internet says that GBS is a disease that attacks at random, no reason, sometimes associated with a touch of flu (or even a flu shot), it takes out the control of muscles and respiration and voice but rarely touches the heart, spine or brain. GBS is one of the MS family of diseases along with ALS (Lou Gehrig disease). The good news is that 100% functional recovery is pretty normal. The bad news is that it usually takes four or five months and more to leave the hospital and longer still to get back full energy, even up to over a year. Cases vary. Entry fitness level and attitude during the illness are key variables. Some, who have given up hope at the onset, have died. Loss of hope depletes the will to live.

It is a rare disease, fewer than one in 100,000 contract it. Some cases see the GBS only attack part of the body. This case was severe, whole body except for a faint movement of the toes and head.

April 1 was not as foolish as it has been in the past. This was no laughing matter. Appointments were cancelled as was the surprise birthday party for my fiftieth, scheduled for April 8. The actual birthday (April 4) was memorable but not in the way all had planned. Carmen and Cathy were called. They kept their flight plans made for the party for themselves and for me. Barb was fielding phone calls and inquiries from many and was becoming weary.

First dream – "Submit"

I was "deep" into the disease. I started to have very vivid dreams. I felt as if I was in a hole, like down a sewer or storm drain, and could only see a small light way above me, as if the light was from street level and I could hear talking from far away. The water in the hole was up to my chin. I was fighting it. Then a movie screen appeared, wide like at IMAX, and the word "submit" slowly scrolled across from right to left. It was not a demand but a question. I considered my options in this well of water. I made a conscious decision and said, "I submit." What I was submitting to was not totally clear but I had the sense that it was the Divine who had asked the question, so talk about free will. I could have said no and left the planet, or so I surmised. Having said yes, the future was not revealed but at least I had one to begin anticipating. I knew then that I would not die. I relaxed and it was suddenly so much easier. My "fight" subsided and I slept.

A man may have never entered a church or a mosque, nor performed any ceremony, but if he realizes God within himself, and is thereby lifted above the vanities of the world, that man is a holy man, a saint, call him what you will…
—*Vivekananda*

I was releasing anger. A good thing. This kind of image message was a new experience. While in the dream it had my total awareness. I experienced it as if in a completely awake, conscious state, yet was almost comatose. I was in the middle rows of the theater but was so absorbed by the image of those letters slowly scrolling across that huge screen that I can't tell you whether or not there were others in the theater with me. Somehow it was simply clear that this was a Divine message, that it was gentle and that I had the option to take it or leave it. That I was in a physically helpless state and relying on machines and nurses to keep me alive was not lost on me. If I say "no," I just slip away. That was not a fearful thought, just felt like the truth. As I recall, it was not a big dramatic moment but just a moment of choice, simple choice.

To "submit," though, meant to do what I am here on earth to do. I didn't know exactly what that was but did have the sense that whatever it was, I hadn't done it yet. I also had the sense that I needed to get on with it, that it was important enough to use GBS to get my attention on it. Yikes.

So a bit of responsibility – well, a lot of responsibility – but to do exactly what I didn't know and too, a bit of curiosity – OK, a lot of curiosity – plus some anticipation of adventure had me come out of the theater and out of the well. Again, sleep.

Is it possible that all dreams have such gravity? How does one get that kind of full-on clarity from a dream? I am thinking that the Divine is offering Guidance all of the time, as choices. When I am "in my head" I am unlikely to notice that a choice is presented to me. When I am physically awake can I still receive Divine Guidance? I say yes, because I have experienced it. It is as if we are on a great path to happiness and fulfillment and to doing something important for the world, and there are signposts along the way. Follow the signs and things go pretty good. Some of the signs may show us the less-than-idyllic event that we need to experience in order to gain the clarity, the wisdom, to allow us to travel the next leg of the journey. Guidance is not only going to show "nice" stuff. It is going to show "needed" stuff, the places of our greatest need to learn, some of which may not feel like fun. Refuse to follow, expect an unhappy journey.

If I have a question that has two possible answers and I flip a coin, while the coin is in the air, that answer, the right or best, answer, often pops into my mind. When I am standing at a buffet table with all those different foods, if I pause and simply look at the table, the food that is best for me at the moment self-identifies and I can "see" which items to put on my plate. I also somehow know how much of each item to spoon on. I say these are examples of Guidance being made available to me. Note that if I stay in my head, only use intellect and book knowledge, ignore my "spidey sense," that the answers are not available, because they are hidden by the yak-yak of my internal know-it-all and critic. I need to be fully present to the Guidance.

One way to find the stillness to hear Guidance to is to attract GBS, a method I do not recommend. When overtaken by the GBS, there is an abundance of focus available because you can't do anything physical.

Another way is to practice "listening" beyond with just the ears. Temporarily detach from the physical world. Become still, focus within, remove any attention to things outside of myself. This is like dousing, the method that one uses to find water with a divining rod. Interesting name for that rod. Dousing for information/insight is most often done with a pendulum, could be anything tied to the end of a string. I don't direct the pendulum. It informs me. But how? When I become still and ask the question, the pendulum swings in the direction to indicate a yes or a no. This is a window to "the other side," a use of "the force," that underlying power and knowing of the Universe. It is the subconscious that is moving the pendulum. The subconscious is tapped into the universal subconscious mind, where all knowledge exists, available for the asking. Wow. No this is not witchcraft, but rather tapping into the All. Btw, the All wants us to know It better. We are welcomed to connect with All.

NEVER MIND PRAYING
FOR LESS PAIN?

April 2 was also a "deep" day but one of waiting rather than fear, and I thought about meaning and what to pray for, if anything. I considered the question, "If I lose a finger, am I still here?" And then, "If I lose an entire limb or even all of my limbs, am I still here?" My conclusion was that I am the same, even without any of my body parts. If that was so then am I still here, even without my body? I surmised that I am not my body and that I do exist even without my body. Having come to that conclusion, I had no need to pray for less pain or to hasten healing or anything at all to do with the body. It is a thing of the earth and thus is a part of time. I figured the body was going as fast as it could with the restrictions of the world upon it. The disease had been beaten the moment I chose to submit. My body was told that and I believed it, so only time was now needed.

They say that we are all being "groomed" for something great and big and worthy. They say that every experience is an attempt to bring us onto that sacred path of "Purpose/Calling."

I was not in a reflective open mood at this point, and yet, this, truly, is the only relevant question, "What is this grooming me for?" I have always, even as a youngster, somehow sensed this idea that everything that showed up as a "You need to get through this" was a part of the learning I needed for some yet unknown something. Something big and important that I would one day discover.

I used this sense to get me through many school/university experiences. I attended (am not quite sure I can fairly use the word "participated") my first round of learning institutions in Alberta, Canada, where, at the time I was fourteen-ish and in grade 9, we all across the province wrote the same departmental exams. I earned all As except for a C in English. Why? Because I had decided that I wanted to be an engineer to invent stuff and to convert sunlight into the solutions the world needed. So I somehow came up with the idea that I didn't need English. At some level I just did what I had to do to get to my objective. Arrogant? Sure, I was fourteen, so I knew everything.

Same kind of thing happened when much later I returned to university to earn a master's degree. All fabulous grades but Cs in the two courses I had to take because my thesis supervisor loved those topics. Blah.

I wonder how long the question "submit" had been playing in that theater? I wonder too, is it still playing? Is that my message, or does it apply to others as well? I can be one stubborn guy, which has gotten me in trouble many times. If I had somehow received the option of that message earlier, I wonder what would have been different. Paired with that thought is whether I could have understood and embraced the message without the prior bumps along my path of life to that point.

A BETTER PRAYER

I finally decided to pray the question, "What is the lesson I am to learn from this experience?" What a wonderful feeling of relief came to me as I formed the prayer for the first time. I actually felt happy and the bodily inconvenience of all this GBS stuff was no longer of import. I was on the recovery path now. I had the thing beat, I knew its number, it was only time that was needed now.

This was a strange kind of relief. Something I didn't remember having experienced before. It seemed that I was connected to Source, almost having a conversation with It, like we were long time confidantes. Like I said, didn't remember having this experience before. It felt very secure, safe, easy. Does it not say somewhere that if one looks upon the face of God, they will die? I'm still here and what kind of god would kill their own creation just for looking at them? Feels like something the ego would make up.

The longtime confidantes idea bears comment. As I grow along here, I find an increasing feeling of camaraderie with Divine. Arrogant? Yes, for that little yakky voice of mine. It goes nuts when I suggest such a thing. Yet, there is a part of me that feels relieved and a kind of "finally" sentiment releases within me. Is not the parent relieved and sincerely grateful when the wayward child returns? Did not the father leap for joy and throw a party when the prodigal son came back? If it is possible to conceive of doing such a thing in our human existence, how much more could this idea be possible in the Divine realm where there is only love?

STILL THE DAD

Barb and Leslie told me that Carmen and Cathy were coming in on the red-eye and I would see them tomorrow. I cried and thanked them. Then I wondered what I could possibly do to let them know that it was OK.

This was a role reversal. I was the helpless one and they were able and fit and had all the physical choices. But I was the Dad and had the idea that I needed to take care of them. Well, this was a challenge that I could not have anticipated and I was feeling helpless in a new way, not just physical, but also in an overwhelming and weird way because I could not even talk. What is a father supposed to do? I was not able to "do" anything. So now what?

Guidance offered the word "reassurance." I could somehow reassure them that all would be fine, that this is but a temporary inconvenience. The dream and my agreement, choice, to submit, was a firm contract with the Divine. I knew it was all just a matter of time but how would I explain my confidence to them. How could I transfer my assurance? I had to make the message light, delivered with smiling eyes and absolute confidence. Yes, that became the plan.

When one is paralyzed and not used to having this Guidance partner so audible there is a lot of confusion. I didn't know what it was all about and was guessing my way along. I made up that it was working and therefore had nothing but evidence that indeed it was working and well.

Barb had started to email people updates on the situation. This out of self-defense from all the phone inquiries and thus needing to repeat the status of things over and over.

> > > -----Original Message-----
> > > **From:**   John
> > > **Sent:**   Friday, March 31, 2000 11:38 AM
> > > **To:**   Barb Seiler
> > > **Subject:**   FW: GBS

Barb:

Sometime, when you feel up to it, Amanda, Darren's wife would be happy to chat with you and perhaps add some insight into how GBS impacts someone with it. Also, if you would like, I would be happy to monitor Joe's daily file here and send home anything that looks like it could be personal or require some attention.

Regards

John

From: Barb Seiler
Sent: Sunday, April 02, 2000 3:44 PM
To: John
Subject: RE: GBS

Thanks John. I appreciate the information and by all means monitor Joe's file.

I have spoken to Amanda, already - she called me and it was good to speak with her.

Joe is doing quite well. Yesterday, they adjusted his respirator so that he is breathing partially on his own and today he said he can sort of swallow! which he was very pleased about. He still can't move but he appears in good spirits although who can really know for sure. We told him Carmen and Cathy would be here tomorrow and he cried. Everyone has been wonderful and I'm sure all the positive energy that is being sent to him is certainly helping his recovery.

Will keep you posted.

Barb

SECOND DREAM –THE BALES

Monday was better in many ways. I was out of "the hole" and my entire psyche was greatly improved. I didn't know anything for sure except that it would all pass. I experienced the first of a particular recurring dream that showed what looked like bales of recycled paper on two pallets, one piled with more bales than the other. There was a bale alone on the top of the higher pile and the number 17 seemed to appear in a pattern on the side of the bale. There was another bale on the floor in front and it had the number 14. A bale on top of the lower pile showed the number 19. Another bale seemed to appear from time to time sort of floating above and in front of it all and it showed the number 28, but it was an intermittent picture, sometimes appearing to show 27 instead of 28.

When a dream shows up again and again, as this one did, it means something, something important. I noticed the dream. Not much choice as it kept on showing itself, like a continuous re-run. Initially, it was not much more than a curiosity since I had not yet figured out what it was saying. Dream interpretation is some kind of strange art. If the dream shows me as a guest on the Ellen show, well that seems clear enough. But this? Those pallets and bales moved into the view by themselves, no fork lift or people, they just sort of floated in and placed themselves into my awareness. Again, I became focused, really attentive to the signals being sent. The movie in the well, the agreement to "submit," seemed to have me looking for what is to come, this something that I had agreed to experience. So I was looking for the Guidance now. That is something I had not done much of in the past. What had I been missing by not purposely looking? How was I supposed to know to look? How would I recognize a bona fide message? Did I need some particular experience or maturity or something before recognition of the messages was even possible?

Normal doubt or skepticism, I suppose. We don't talk about such things much, or at least haven't until the last few decades or so. As a species, we have been busy evolving past the flight-or-fight responses of our primordial ancestors. As we awaken and start to experience the presence of Source and cautiously start to acknowledge that this is what it might actually be, well, it is an exciting time. I have been the left-brained model for most of my life. With the noticing of these kinds of new age possibilities, I have certainly opened my right brain and have become a bona fide "seeker," one who seeks the Divine. I had released anger, didn't need to bargain because I thought I had a great deal, so skipped past depression into Acceptance. Amazing stuff.

I received some select visitors and felt optimistic. The nurse offered that it was OK for me to be angry, but I wasn't. She almost insisted that it was OK and that I should show it. I smiled. She didn't know what I knew. It was over.

My only means of communication was by moving my eyes. I would spell by blinking the letters of the alphabet. The hard part was when the one I was spelling for would forget the first word when we were part way through the message. Or they would forget and mix up letters before we even got to the end of the word. Now that was frustrating.

Carmen and Cathy arrived straight from the airport before noon, a little bleary-eyed, but intent on finding out what all of this was about. The nurses had found an alphabet chart that I could "point" at with my eyes and spell to communicate. I had prepared. Cathy held the paper while I spelled, "I am strengthened by our love. Only my body is unhappy." It seemed to have a calming effect. We chatted a while and it was good to be together.

I had wanted to have a big birthday party once in my life and had asked some years ago that it be my fiftieth. Tuesday, April 4 was the actual birthday. I received a very significant present that day. I had an operation to install a tracheotomy tube, allowing me to get rid of the tubes installed up to now through my mouth. I hadn't closed my mouth or fully swallowed for over five days. It was a wonderful improvement. The more traditional gifts would not be opened for some time.

From: Barb Seiler
Sent: Tuesday, April 04, 2000 9:31 AM
To:
Subject: RE: GBS

We are having our ups and downs. He was supporting himself somewhat but since developing pneumonia - an expected complication, he has had a lot of congestion in his right lung. However, it was less yesterday than the day before. Today they have him scheduled for a trachea - something to replace the respirator - he still needs support but this is supposed to be more comfortable and will make things a bit easier for him. His spirits are good and the nurse thought he was less frustrated yesterday than the day before. Physio comes regularly to work with him. He likes that - he says it doesn't hurt - but it is terribly exhausting for him.

Just leaving for the hospital now - will keep you posted.

Barb

When I was nine Mom allowed me to have a birthday party and invite all my favorite friends from school. I was in grade 4 and invited eleven people. We were not exactly well off, so this was a very big deal.

Not one of them showed up. Only one of them acknowledged their absence when I was back at school on Monday. It was a tough thing to understand and my wish for a real birthday party "once in my life," I believe, may have been fueled by that distant past event. Who knows? What does the mind of a nine-year-old make up about all eleven friends not showing up? This idea of my carrying that experience in my body and in my memory for decades was brought to my attention by a colleague. She showed me how to bring the event forward and to address it with my adult mind. Hmmm? What a thing, huh.

Day 7, April 4. I had not moved my bowels since entering the hospital, almost a week earlier. Even with a suppository and an enema it took about four exhausting hours to gain the much-needed relief. I had, a few days before, set myself a goal of drinking a glass of cool water. With the breathing tube entering my neck instead of going down my throat, that was now possible. Mmmmm, it was good to drink again. When Leslie arrived to visit I was able to spell, "I can swallow and poop." It was a wonderful day! Time to set another goal. The image of the frosted glass of water had sustained me for over two days. I wanted to talk.

From: Barb Seiler
Sent: Tuesday, April 04, 2000 9:31 AM
To:
Subject: RE: Flowers and stuff

Flowers are not allowed in intensive care, but can be sent after he is on a regular type ward. Cards, however, can be sent anytime. If people want to send them to me - I will take them in and read them to him. He seems to enjoy that. People can even email their wishes and I will read those to him also.

17 Manchester Drive
Stillwater Lake, NS
B3Z 1G9

THIRD DREAM – THE ARBOR

I had another recurring dream start about this time. I could see an arbor, in black, about fifteen feet away against a dark sky but with a sliver of light on the horizon, as if pending dawn. There was some source of light off to the left behind me as if from a great city at night. Someone was with me and we were looking at the arbor. It was on a path that I seemed to have just traveled. There were yellow tongues of flame all around the closer side of the arbor and an arm that looks like a large leaf with jagged flame edges on the exit side (nearer side) of the arbor. I was standing with "another" to my right and slightly behind me. I was dressed in a soft tan robe with a hood and my face was not visible. The hood and the large sleeve were trimmed in a darker brown. My legs appeared nearly stick-like and only a stick-like hand protruded from the sleeves. My hands were horizontal from the elbow.

It felt like we were quietly pondering the passage through the arbor and that it was a good thing to have done. A shadow of someone struggling, someone large, passed right to left across the path between us and the arbor. They seemed to be working hard and almost as if dragging or carrying a great weight toward the city.

What did it mean? Maybe the arbor was the disease experience. Maybe the "other" being was my Guide or Protector or Angel. Maybe the person passing was a reminder that we each have our own journey and for some it is hard and for some not so hard. Maybe it meant nothing at all.

The arbor with the large flaming leaf was something that I had walked through. A rite of passage, maybe? The flaming leaf did not burn but the edges of the leaf, it seemed, were razor sharp and dangerous. That I appeared so gaunt, barely skin and bone, remains strange as I had not lost that much weight yet. It strikes me now that I had a long ways to "grow into." That was a more likely meaning for that imagery. Or maybe not. My journey of learning was just beginning. I knew only enough to have survived in life up to this time. I was barely alive in the Spiritual sense. I had enough "life" to stand and to walk away from the arbor. My Guide was with me (recognized as such for the first time in my memory) and it was dawn. So a full day ahead and I felt supported, protected and ready, though unsure of what was to come. As days start at midnight, I had been through the darkest hour and possibly had, by passing through the arbor, by agreeing to submit, been prepared to meet the light of the full day. I feel like that now. Funny to feel like that, ready, even though I am not able to tell you what I am ready for. Just ready, ready for whatever it is that is next, like learning to skate and then one day joining a hockey team. That first time on the ice with a uniform on and all those other guys who know what to expect, yikes, exhilarating and scary stuff that I had not anticipated and now that it is happening, loving it.

Two kinds of learning

Man's search for meaning? Sounds familiar, book title by Victor Frankl, and feels a familiar theme. My own penchant for understanding is powerful, I am told. I really like to understand things and will be like a dog on a pant leg asking, clarifying, asking some more until the aha shows up. I can be selfish in this way. That aha … I am thinking it is more of a "now I remember, and yes this is right" instead of "I have now learned something all new and I now see how it works." There is quite a difference in the two outcomes from discovery. Part of the difference comes from a different approach to the discovery process.

Is it not so that in things of logic and of the physical, that we can be shown/taught and eventually "see how it works" for the first time? I propose that in things of the Spirit, for instance "How does love work?" it is the remembering kind of aha that we experience. The kind of aha that feels familiar, even if distantly familiar, is often my experience and it is the kind of aha that comes from Guidance. An attribute of Guidance is that one submits to simply asking the questions and trusting the answers given. I don't mean blindly accepting answers but "allowing" that what is given as answer "might" indeed be so. And the ones that feel familiar, even if not crystal clear just yet, we are invited to consider, not discharged and tossed out completely just because I don't quite get it yet.

These are learned behaviors. I am "seeking" now for answers to Spirit-based learning, so I find myself remembering more than learning for the first time. It is a choice and I am so glad to have taken this path. One summary of this might be that it is my ego that wants to, sometimes demands to, understand (a kind of fear-based demand to learn). This other kind of learning comes from curiosity seeking Guidance where even the question is guided. I, as do you, have a "something" that I am to learn during my lifetime. That something that I don't know in advance but will recognize when I encounter it. Encountering the aha that feels familiar is subtle (can't hear the b in subtle but it is indeed still there). I need to sense it, rather than hear it in the usual manner.

Important distinctions here. How did I get to sensing instead of a steady diet of listening and seeing in the physical? My recollection is that I had a moment here and a moment there, where what I came upon just felt worth exploring more, regardless of how off the wall it seemed at the time of initial discovery. This concept of remembering rather than learning in the schoolbook sense is an example of one of these things. I accumulated a felt sense about something like this and one day, in coaching a client, I noticed and named an aha the client had shared as, "Oh wow, seems like you remember that, how familiar does it feel to you?" The response was a resounding "Yes, remember and yes, familiar," and wow, how did you know that? For some time after, I thought on that blurt of mine. My discovery of what I now know to be true had begun.

It is not uncommon for me now to ask a client, "How much of that feels remembered (familiar)?"

THE CREAMED COFFEE DREAM

Thursday, April 6

I had a dream and a then recurring image of myself and someone who reminded me of one of my friends. The colors of the images were all a shade of a soft light tan, like coffee with a lot of cream in it. The only exception was my friend's head. Her hair and face were normal colors and more distinct than the blur of the rest of the scene. Our bodies were only just visible as the shadows created by the shape and movement of muscles. Everyone had glistening, almost invisible, wings with silver accents here and there on our bodies. There were many other pairs but I could not see any faces but hers and hers was not totally clear. We were dancing and touching at the hands. In the dancing, which was very soft and easy, flowing and graceful, the beings sometimes passed right through each other, as if they/we were some sort of vapor. I felt as if I was a part of some heavenly ocean with all the other beings connected to me through the liquid. I asked Barb to call my friend so that I might see her. I later learned that the church ladies had gotten together to pray for me and am now surmising that this image was a result of that prayer and the one similarity to a person I knew was but coincidence.

We make things up. We want to "get it" even when what we make up, which we decide needs to be understood, is not a truth. I suppose that it is more comforting to think we know something in a strange scene, to ascribe some kind of meaning to it. Now that I review this dream it is more clearly about we, us humans, all being a part of something live and large and vibrant and that we are inseparable from that. We are that. Also, at the level I was at in that dream, we were all very happy, at ease, gentle, just flowing and basking, yes that's it, basking in the presence of each other and whatever It was/is that held/holds us there. Ego was not present. Therefore, there was nothing akin to fear or any of fear's cousins. As I now attempt to "go there" I feel a freshness, purity and easiness and a soft smile comes of itself. Wow, I just thought of the idea of going there this minute and a part of me is there now as I write these words. It is not that common to feel completely safe, yet re-entering this strange image brings the feeling of total safety. What might it be like to feel so safe all of the time? What is in my way from having that feeling at least more often?

What would it take to bring people into this state where it feels so safe, so very safe? Is this the place, maybe one of many, where ego holds no power over me? It feels like it. Try it yourself. I welcome you to close your eyes and to feel a gentle, safe, lightness and flow where you are like a droplet in the sea, part of it, inseparable from it, yet still distinct somehow. It is not that one gives oneself up to be a part of this sea. It is that the sea is the result of many giving of themselves to each other.

At this moment, indescribably, effortlessly, home.

Many, giving of themselves to each other. We form this sea. This sea is accessible below our conscious level of thought. It is not quite "a place" but more of "a state" of submission. When I allow myself to <u>submit</u> to this sea I am in the safe embrace of Source. I am Source. Too much? Maybe. And what if it is so, even though a bit tough to conceive of? Time to "what if" and to release knowing the logic of this possibility. If I didn't have to know the logic, what might I allow into my thinking and exploring here? It is "something" because I do feel a different kind of embrace from this place, this sea.

And I must note the use of the word "submit."

Body and Observer

From: Barb Seiler
Sent: Thursday, April 06, 2000 9:57 AM
To: list
Subject: Joe

Joe is slowly regaining some muscle movement, but he still has very little strength. He has started a second series of immunoglobulin (I think that's the spelling) for the next five days. His spirits are good. His respirator support was changed on Tuesday night so that the respirator is connected directly to his airway through the throat rather than through the mouth. This makes him much, much more comfortable. Now he can move his lips to speak (still can't talk). I just need to learn how to lip-read! He's expected to remain in ICU for at least another week. It all depends on when he can breathe on his own, without respirator support.

Will keep in touch

Barb

Communication was much easier once I could form letters and words with my lips. I had to entertain myself in unusual ways, as I still could not move much. I had decided to further test this "I am not a body" idea. I received needles to draw blood daily and they always put a nice big tape over the hair on my arm after and then pulled it off the next day. The changes in the IV needle site was not as often but when they did that one, it was a much bigger tape to be removed. Do you think they could shave a guy first? Not a chance.

So I decided that I would no longer feel any pain when they removed those tapes. It took about three tries to achieve it, but I managed to get to the point where I indeed did not feel the tapes being removed. I managed to maintain that state for about four days. The mind really does tell the body what to do. I was very glad of it in this case.

I am learning, no, remembering, that I am not my body. My body is an antenna that is stimulated by both the physical and the spirit worlds.

Where am "I" in this picture? The body picks up the stimulus and makes a phone call to the brain which, based on experience, maybe some rules of thumb and a library of data (something I read on the internet or overheard in the Starbucks line-up), decides on a response to the stimulus. What feels true is that I am somehow observing all of this, but only when I am present to the scene unfolding. Like I am in the balcony watching the scene on the stage and, guess what, I am always one of the main characters in the play that I am watching. Also, I get to slow time down and direct/ inform the "me" that is on that stage. The other very important possibility is that the brain may have turned the phone off. Oh, oh.

An even more amazing thing is that I can leave my seat in the balcony, go out to the washroom or the concessions or outside and, amazing thing of amazing things, the play keeps on going without any direction from me. Well, not from the me that is objective and seeing the entire stage and who has a copy of the programme with the storyline somewhat explained. Direction, in this case, is coming from the "me" that is on the stage, can't see the overall picture, so makes up the data that is missing from that lower plane of view. The "thinker" in this case is mostly the ego, an emotionally immature five-year-old who is afraid of, well, everything. Hmmm? Well, let us wonder what is happening, or could be happening on the stage with the balcony Observer, who can direct from that higher view, absent. I have been that. When I describe this scene, who comes to mind as having their Observer spending a lot of time in their foyer while their play continues without their input? People live life this way sometimes, I mean besides you and me.

Entering the view plane of Observer does magic things. For starters, I am detached from that annoying little internal critic, that voice that just won't leave me alone. Nice. That voice is in the "me" that is on the stage, not the "me" that is in the balcony watching it all. I get to listen to the yak-yak and maintain my choice whether or not to believe what it is saying to me. Because the Observer can bend time, I can slow things down, roll things ahead a few hours or days or months, even years, to explore the possible results of choices. I get to pretest options. How cool is that?

If, in my observing, I notice fear (or any of its many cousins) then I am well advised to check my vantage point. Am I on the stage or in the balcony? Am I in my body and have I decided that my body experience is real or not real? The ability to float around, into and out of, any of these points of view is available to all of us. All that is needed is a willingness to try it. I was watching a mini-series where the teacher at a school for blind children was struggling to get a new student to try anything that was proposed, whether that was using a knife and fork to eat their own meals or how to get around the school unaided. The student refused, citing many reasons why they were unable to do such things. Their main reason was, of course, that they were now blind. The main blocker was the thinking that the student, having lived life with sight until now, didn't know much about the new methods being offered so rejected them outright. Since he would not accept the possibility of the new ways, he simply sat, blind.

I am offering some different ways to access levels of knowing that not many of us occupy very often. In order to experience what I suggest, foregoing and to come, we are invited to become like a newly blinded person who is willing to try different approaches. No, we are not newly blinded, but with respect to these unusual kinds of knowing, might we not be moving toward greater clarity, coming out of a kind of blindness? Some are anxious eager and ready and willing, right now. Some are on the fence. I'm so excited that I am more than willing. Without that willingness there will only be stasis. I want more than stasis. I suggest, also, that if people do not try to access other layers of awareness, there will be darkness, unnecessary darkness. I have found myself in this position many times. I have come to call it the place of "I know." When "I know" there is not a chance that anything will teach me, because I have decided that I know, so don't try to teach what I already know, period. I stop seeing or hearing. Stasis. My experience.

They put me into a special chair for a while. It was a dizzy episode for me, having been totally horizontal for so long. I got Barb to take a picture with me and the girls, sorta like

45

Christopher Reeves, with the trach and all. Part of my attempt to make it all a little less scary. Who takes pictures of someone full of tubes in the intensive care unit? Well, we did and it was a good thing to do.

Notice the ego making things hard again. Here I am, barely able to move my body and my ego-driven mind makes up that I am going to somehow "save" my family by demonstrating some lies. Wow. Or let's go the other way, "My true purpose in life is to show how the body is a mere vehicle that my superior mind controls. See, watch this." If those aren't ego taking hold of the steering wheel, what is? And it is nothing at all if not funny to notice the machinations and squirms of the ego. I am learning to laugh at it, to give up the disease of "seriousness" that used to take me over so often. Oh yes, I still get serious, just not as serious, darkly serious, and certainly not as often.

It is a new way of interacting with the world and I absolutely love it way better. When I released the seriousness and responsibility of being the Dad and the husband I could be fun and indeed, from that platform of enjoying a situation like the one I was in, I guess I did add some lightness and soften the fear around it all. So this balance between the two teeter-tottered along day by day. It was not what I was doing as much as it was the source of the motivation. When I did what I did from the less serious plane, better things happened. I felt better.

Another way to look at it is to notice that I got scared when the dizziness came on like a freight train. Valid? Yes. I think the threat of puking my guts out, and doing that in front of everyone whom I thought was convinced I was the guy in the picture I had so diligently been painting – conquering hero – was just too much for my ego. The ego knows, even probably invented, fear. So I experienced a big dose of being human. Nothing broken, but now better understood. I'm fine (or at least better) now. Well, as one dear friend used to say, "mostly fine."

Three steps to better

1. Having an ego experience is not "wrong". It is what we have come to earth to experience. So if I notice one, well, applaud. Having noticed, that is the hugest step one.

2. Then get in there and ask, what is the name of this that I have noticed? This is a fabulous step two.

3. Now, step three is to choose what to do with it all. Do I believe and act on the claim of the ego? Or something else? Usually, sometimes not, the something else is a happier choice, so choose toward greater happiness and get on with enjoying life. Done.

Notice, name, choose

In the movie Million Dollar Baby, the boxing coach (Clint Eastwood) uses a great little technique to open his fighters to reality and useful action. The fighter (Hillary Swank) is getting clobbered. Coach lists the assets the other fighter has over her, more experienced, younger, faster, etc., and then ends with

"What are you going to do about it?" She goes out and with one punch knocks her opponent out. This three-step sequence is like that. Notice, name, choose toward a better result. Then go for the knockout that serves your greater happiness. With a little bit of practice, you never know, you could find yourself triumphant over situations that used to beat you up. I say try it. Start with Observer. Even if that is as far as one gets, life will be better.

And let us upgrade the foregoing comments about learning to "What can I remember here?" Now that is rocket fuel for sure. The main indicator of "remembering" versus learning is that the aha feels somehow familiar. That feeling of familiar needn't be overwhelming or "like a freight train" – only the ego demands that sort of splash. Just pause and tune in to yourself. Feel even mildly familiar? Done. If not, shrug and move on.

Would it be OK to let myself "remember" what I notice? Or do I demand that I know it like I know book learning? Try just remembering. When I remember, a lot of details get filled in all of a sudden. No need to go back to the textbook or the teacher. Just let the picture fill out some.

I know, sounds too simple. Just because I don't think it is so, or think it needs to be some more or some less of something or another, does not mean it isn't so. The other side of the coin is also vital to understand. The lawyer asks a question, knowing it will be "Objection, your Honor!" and the objection will be sustained, the court secretary instructed to strike the offending question from the record. Having asked it, the idea is now planted with the jury and that was all the lawyer intended. Our imagining mind adds all kinds of made-up detail. We love lurid innuendo and conspiracy and catching the uppity-ups with their pants down or with their hand in the cookie jar.

OK, let's use that human tendency to plant the seed of "If it feels even mildly familiar, it might just be true." Sort of like delicious gossip. We can't let it go and our imagination toys with the gossip and adds all kinds of things that were not there in the original statement. In this case, use that tendency to embellish, to explore beyond the initial aha. This is an important lesson, <u>to allow the possibility that I may be remembering something vital</u> to my greater future. It might also just be indigestion, but let the possibility of more at least exist. What's the rush? Let it sit there as a possibility. Keep an eye on it and let it marinate.

Friday was more of the same incremental progress and nice visits with the family and a few friends. I was tremendously blessed with caring visitors and a seemingly endless stream of cards and emails that Barb would read to me each day. I felt so much a part of a large group, never alone. I was beginning to notice time. I might go two hours without communicating to anyone and that was hard. I am a generally social person. I looked forward to the visit by the physio people who concentrated on strengthening my breathing reflexes and began to move my limbs for me so they wouldn't totally seize up. I enjoyed a lot of play with them too. She was "the physio lady" and he (the student) was "her manservant and enforcer."

There was something almost false about the banter and humor, no, something almost detached, not false, more as if we were all in the scene but also all watching the scene. That might be better than real, way above false. Hmmm? I had a sense they were really glad that they didn't have what I had. Were they a bit nervous about what to do with this guy? Normal stuff, as most people might agree. Since we are here to have experiences, human experiences that include a lot of illusions like death and pain and so forth, that would mean that I can observe my body, etc., while having the experiences. Wouldn't that just heighten the learning, allow the experience to be reviewed as it is happening? Much of this seemed that way. My part in this play was to be cheerful, which wasn't that hard, but my script did not feel like it could include other options, so I was cheerful.

So, if we are here to learn, which I do believe we are, and we notice the learning angle is better when in "observer" or is it Observer, then why not consciously choose to be Observer more often? That is exactly what I have been doing.

I am still most often "in human," in the belief that life is real and that all that happens is also real, that I can die (the forever kind of death that the ego fears so), that the "I" being spoken about here is finite and vulnerable, can be hurt in psychological as well as physical ways, that living in fear is what I am supposed to be experiencing.

Not.

MORE ABOUT OBSERVER

The more time I choose Observer, the greater my conviction that it is all a movie in which a reflection of me plays a part and that my mind simply has an opinion about it all. When the opinion is formed from the platform of Observer, I learn, am reminded, about how it really works. That view is enjoyable in all kinds of ways and often brings a smile. It sometimes brings outright laughter at the alternative "in human" opinion, that I did not choose, and that I can actually "see" from the Observer position. Fun.

To experience Observer, simply watch my thoughts as they float by across my mind. This is way easier than one might guess. It feels to me like I am in a movie that I am watching. My viewpoint is from inside my body, most often my head, as if behind the eyes, and can also be above me, watching me walk down the road or doing whatever it is I am doing at that moment. There are a few really valuable attributes of going to Observer. One is that the I being observed can have an emotion without me, as Observer, being hooked by that emotion. Really valuable when working through something, like, for instance, anger. I feel anger about something that happened with Mary. She dissed me. At least I believe she did, well, my ego has decided to be dissed. So it unfolds if I have chosen to believe what the ego voice is telling me. Wait, what if I had not decided that way but had decided to be neutral about what she said? From anger I can easily go to aggression, revenge, hate, a whole host of toxic feelings fueling not so acceptable actions. The menu is extensive. Now remember that I chose to believe anger was my position on the matter. Wait, back up the train here. If I had chosen neutrality my responses are more likely to be release, trust and just being accepting of Mary's remark/action. That does not mean I like or condone or want to encourage Mary's remark/action. I just accept it without being hooked by it.

Oh sure, you say, easy to write but not easy to do. I agree. Yet, when I have managed to catch myself and choose a less toxic response I have been happier with the result. Can't get there, or at least it is a tougher road to get there, without entering Observer. From Observer time slows down and I really do get to choose my responses. I smile more, laugh more and enjoy life more, not to mention that Mary and I get along better. And notice that there is no part of this that is trying to change Mary. She gets to be and do whatever it is that Mary is and does. However, I assert that if Mary's ego is not getting the reaction that it was trying to get out of me, after a while it will either convince Mary to talk with someone else or will stop using that provoking approach with me. Feels pretty good to me.

One more point. I don't suppress the anger. I feel it, let it sit there but not hook me and then choose a different option from the menu.

I didn't want to bug the nurses for little things, they were so wonderfully patient. My ears were quite hot and sensitive, being laid on so long and not having the ability to even put my hand under my head to relieve what became considerable pressure on the earlobes. I would try to lay with my head perfectly straight not touching either ear to the pillow. Elbows also became hugely sensitive and I did not discover a way to get them away from the coarse – I might say merciless – bed sheets.

Use of the bedpan was a big event. You can see I was desperate for entertainment.

I began to also observe, kind of tune in with, other patients. It seemed that every person had a "state" that they were in and their state moved around as things happened. It was quite different, more calm, when they were not awake or conscious. Why might that have been? Maybe when operating "below" the level of human wakefulness there is less to be anxious about. Maybe it has to do with ego, that fear generator guy, could be resting too and is not playing nasty with one's thoughts. That would also explain the rested rejuvenated feeling we have when we come out of a good sleep. That also fits with the feeling after a deep meditation, where the mind is quieted and at least somewhat separated from the pestering ego. That feels about right.

From: Barb Seiler
Sent: Saturday, April 08, 2000 8:50 AM
To: list
Subject: Joe update

A little more good news. Yesterday and the day before, he was actually able to move (the nurses moved him) to a chair and he was able to sit up for about 45 minutes. It's a lot of work for him to do that, but mentally it's good, and certainly good for his lungs - they can expand more. His movement is slowly increasing - he can wiggle his toes, hips, and shrug his shoulders. Movement in legs and arms is still not there, but overall the doctor says he is pleased with him! Joe says he's pleased with himself, too!

They started him on a second round (5 days) of immunoglobulin and in ten days will do an EMG (electromyography) to see how well the nerves conduct signals.

One nurse said Joe is one of the most pleasant GBS patients she has ever seen.

Our two daughters from out west have been home (here) since Monday, but will be leaving this Monday coming. Joe was really glad to see them and they have been a big help and comfort.

Joe is still expected to stay in ICU a little while longer - I'm hoping it's only days, but bottom line is the respirator. Oh yes, they had him on pressure support yesterday - that means they are trying to wean him off the respirator. He was at a 10 (whatever that means), then they will try 8 and when he reaches 6 he can come off breathing support. He tolerated the pressure support very well yesterday. Sometimes patients go back and forth, off again, on again, the respirator, in the final weaning stages. Each one is different.

All in all, things are progressing incrementally up each day. His spirits are good and I'm sure it is in no small way due to the fact that you all are sending such positive, healing energy in his direction. My deepest thanks.

Barb

Today, thirteen years later, I don't have a solid answer to the question about whether the ego sleeps. My experience is that we do "go deeper" when we sleep and that the ego is not heard bleating and wailing and pestering in the usual way. It can be a factor in dreams with replays of events from the day before or proposed outcomes for events planned to the next day(s). This is a great hint. The ego does not exist in the present moment. It thrives on reliving and twisting past events into fearsome things. It also loves to predict disastrous futures. Both of those are fabrications, use of fearful imagination to bring out our victimhood, that poor-me persona that is terrified of pretty much anything and everything. Those predictions and fears of things that did not happen in the past or at least not in that newly formed way, are not "in time" but outside of time and thus have no dominion over me as I traverse my earthly journey unless I believe them to be true and imagine them happening now.

If I have such dreams then I am not feeling rested when I awake. Bingo. If I had actually fallen into real sleep those dreams would not follow me down the rabbit hole, I'd be rested. My assertion, then, is that ego does not survive the journey to deep sleep. Until I release my thoughts from the control of the yak-yak of my ego I cannot enter deep sleep.

Ever meet a person who has a negative prediction and an attitude of "can't" for every good suggestion? A strong hint that the ego is in control and that the person is not in the present moment. Stressful. How often do I go to that place? How often do you?

Yeah, yeah, so how do I get to that deep sleep place? I use long breath often, also concentrating on what I want (like sleep), going to "meadow," laughing at the thoughts the ego is suggesting are true. Go to sleep laughing, what a recipe. More on this to come.

NOTICING MY WAY THROUGH (THE BODY KNOWS)

S aturday felt quite positive for me, no particular reason. Cathy and I were talking and she commented on how positive my attitude was and had been. I responded with the observation that I had very little control of anything else so that I might as well put my energy into one thing I could control, my attitude. It was serving me well. That moment, with Cathy and Carmen at bedside, was a nice one that I will remember for quite a while. They were much more relaxed than when they had arrived. As I said, it was a good day.

The week was ending and the girls would be leaving soon. But it was OK, somehow. The dream with the numbers was still occurring and I was getting the sense that I would be out of the hospital by around 28 days (that number was still blinking to 27 a bit). I was not sure about the other numbers but had started to guess. I had not yet told anyone about the dream.

My elbows were both very tender by this time. It was a matter of recognizing that since I could not move my arms that the elbow was in touch with the sheet twenty-four hours a day, every day. This paralyzed state has a lot of littler inconveniences that most people would not expect. My left hand was starting to wake up and the relief to the elbow was the first grateful result, once I could move it off the sheet.

Each morning I would inspect and try my body to see what improvement had occurred over night. I was to the point where I could sort of wiggle my middle and if I put my hand on my tummy I could, between wiggling and bouncing, get my left hand up beside my head. It was a real help with the ears. The other thing was that I could now greet people with a wave of my hand beside my head. The best part was when I could then lift my hand and wave on the way up to vertical. Alas, I could not hold the hand up and it would fall down beside my waist with a thump. I say it was still the best part because everyone found it hilarious when the hand, having performed so well up the point of being vertical, would lamely drop to the mattress. As I said, I was desperate for entertainment.

There is something vital in the description of my days at this time. It is in the "noticing" small differences in body ability and that the noticing was made possible because I went looking. The body is a very fine antenna. It picks up signals from the rest of the world. The body knows my hand is on a hot stove before the mind is told. If there were no antenna or no noticing, the right decision could not be made in the mind other than by fluky guess.

As I live my life I am well advised to notice also the signals the body does not detect, the intuition kinds of signals. The intuition is of the soul and heart, and is connected to the universal subconscious mind, the place of all knowing. If intuition speaks I then need to go looking for what the message is for me. Since we don't do this much, aren't taught about it, we may not know how to glean the data from the message in the intuition. I am learning that stillness, both physical and mental, is a great help. I have also learned that the answer may come as another intuitive hit and may need interpretation. Intuition does not always speak English.

Finally, I notice that some intuitive hits invoke a physical companion response (a sinking in my stomach, a spontaneous giggle, a shiver up the spine) This is very good. I can notice an intuitive "something" and even if I don't find a convincing answer to what it may mean, I can check my body and see if there is a companion sensation somewhere. Over time I can accumulate a library of companion meanings and sensations. Helpful.

So we have one route from physical sensation (hot stove top) to mind to "interpretation and understanding" and the other route, from intuitive hit that stimulates a part of the body, thereby to the mind, to "interpretation and understanding." This is all about noticing myself and noticing, in particular, the role the body plays in delivery of "hits."

Here is a method that can really work great. Library that body sensation against that particular intuitive signal. Write down both of these as a match. Keep a record. Also note what is, and has, been going on around you. Won't be too long before a pattern suggests itself. Bingo, you are becoming a master intuitive. Using the body as an early alert signal is a great strategy. I believe we are designed to use those parts of us in this way. I look forward to the day that such methods are taught in schools, and at an early age, please. Life becomes so much more understandable and easy. Happy outcomes become the norm. A good thing.

JOSEPH SEILER

From: Barb Seiler
Sent: Monday, April 10, 2000 3:05 PM
To: list
Subject: Joe update

More good news. Today Joe is on pressure support 6, and when I left the hospital this morning at about 11:00 they were putting him on oxygen (that is no respirator, but oxygen assistance). At 1:00 I called and he was doing well. If he maintains that they may not have to put him back on the respirator and he will be breathing on his own. However, if he gets tired, they can easily switch him back.

He sits daily in the chair now, although still for only short periods of time. He gains more muscle movement and some strength each day. He still is not able to lift his arms or legs by himself, but some pushing strength is obvious in his legs and he can squeeze your hand with his fingers.

Such little things - that we mostly do unconsciously and take for granted, all of a sudden become life's miracles!

I don't know yet what the next step is after he gets out of ICU - which is likely to be a few more days yet.

Joe thanks you all for your thoughts and prayers.

Will be in touch.

Barb

GETTING ANSWERS

What does a person do when the mind is so alert and ready to rock'n'roll but the body is barely able to move? I did a lot of internal reflection, tested some theories and did some experiments with thought and with body sensation. I became fascinated at how connected the mind and body are and how disconnected they could be, just by my choosing to connect or disconnect. That brought me to the whole question of, if I am watching the body and watching the mind, where am I? I found huge spacious "places" and, believe it or not, company – well, I didn't feel alone. I felt held and supported and absolutely safe. It was like this benevolent group of beings were all around me with their only role to be caring toward me, to encourage me and to smile toward me constantly. I can both see and feel that crowd now, just by thinking of them and I am now smiling more broadly because of it.

So ... maybe I could think of them, remember their presence, more of the time and thus feel supported and encouraged and smiled at, loved, more of the time. I like that. The other benefit is the feeling of safety and loss of anything like urgency. There is no stress whatsoever when I place myself inside this group. Things are just "as is" and there are no concerns of any kind. Yet, it does not feel lazy, not as though I (we) are just loafing around wherever it is that I find myself in these "spaces." It feels like we are just bathing in love and that there are no demands, no time, no need to work or eat or diet or compete, no demands at all. Feels more than nice. It feels "eternal and infinite" and how cool is that.

I spoke of intuitive hits a few pages back. These last few paragraphs came from intuition. I did not know I would write them when I started to type today. And I "remember" the truth of it. It is familiar and it is true and it is available to all of us, anytime. Nice.

Our two eldest daughters returned home to Calgary and Vancouver. At least they left their Dad on a clearly positive path and pretty happy too. Their presence for that week was wonderful. They helped me greatly, strengthening my resolve and cheering me along.

I was breathing close to on my own. My spirits were up and each day gave me a new gift of the return of one or more muscles back to my control. I was weak in the extreme but to have the sensation of muscle control returning was like having a front row seat at the creation of mankind. Day by day, functionality returned. I was asked by the nurses, and especially by the physio team, to "show me what you can do today." Well, ever the showman, I looked forward to the daily demonstrations and hammed it up while I was at it. This part was actually fun, reinforcing the message of recovery and keeping my spirits fueled.

The dream with the black arbor and flames was still there but my viewpoint was more distant, not the fifteen feet or so from the initial dream. It was receding into the distance and the sky was getting brighter, like a new dawn. I could still see myself, or the shell of the cloak I had worn, in the picture still dutifully looking at the arbor from fifteen feet away. The "other being" who had been beside me originally seemed to have become blurry. I took it that the passage through the flames on the arbor was the disease and the distance confirmed my earlier sense that it was gone and beaten.

What's the formula, the method? How do we do these trips to these "spaces"? I think we do it automatically but at a different level than the waking level. "Oh, great," you say, so how do we get the message out to where our conscious mind can recognize it? That is the question now.

As I ask that of myself I feel compelled to print off a copy of a table from Power vs Force by Hawkins. The table shows a map of consciousness with the feeling of "shame" as the lowest conscious level (when Adam and Eve left the garden they felt shame and sought to cover themselves). The levels climb through seventeen plateaus to "enlightenment," which is pure consciousness, no body effects at all. When I live normally, I depend a lot on my body. Have to, in order to survive and thrive in an earthly existence. But in my state in that hospital ICU, my body was not much available and by accident or maybe default, I seemed to have capacity or something like that, to access a higher energy level, a higher level of consciousness. In that higher state many of the things that are not accessible in my prior normal living situations became ordinary. It was not that I asked for the images, they just showed up. Their meaning was for me to decide, no text to explain them. And I couldn't do it wrong, either. It was all made available like a Divine buffet of some magical kind.

As I now write this I recall many experiences of some kind of "hit" coming to me not long after meditation or while on my run in the outdoors. Are these the same or at least of the same family? These are mild by comparison, but certainly similar. As I progressed through the stages of "coming back" the dreams stopped. Hmmm? So I believe that I have been provided "hits" for all of my life, that I sense them when I am in a higher energy level (per the Power vs Force table).

At this moment, as I write, I am feeling a bit stuck to answer the question, "How do I access that kind of knowing?" The knowing hits I was getting in these states of "stillness" were strong and indelible messages. Whether or not I could understand them as presented was another matter.

So I had set aside the writing of this book to go and "research" or just ponder some on that question. Within a few days, to my dismay, I was again in the hospital, physically, really, in January of 2013, nearly thirteen years after contracting GBS.

I had GBS again.

More on the details of that chapter in my life later. I received the answer to "How do I access that kind of knowing?"

The answer is in that old saying, "Seek and ye shall find." The answers are always present to all of us, just need to get still and go looking to find them. Or is it that I need to let the answers in? I was again paralyzed with a bright, active, mind so applied myself to "asking" for the answer. Divine helped me to "see" that the answer is always around and in me, and in you, and that I but need to subdue the opinion that speaks so loudly when I first notice a "something" that I call a soft intuitive hit. "Soft," meaning that it is not one of those baseball bat hits-in-the-side-of-the-head ahas. Just a soft whisper in amongst the many thoughts floating around all the time. Our mind does not stop generating thoughts. Thousands and thousands each and every day. Never mind that the overwhelming majority are the exact same as yesterday, very few original thoughts. It is in those few original thoughts that the completely clear and recognizable, true answers are found. My job is to ask for answers and to allow them to come into my awareness. Unanswered questions develop some disquiet which then generate – or is it invite? – a response. If I am not letting answers into my awareness I can develop a discomfort in my body as a signal to pay attention, message incoming. Hmm?

The biggest problem in doing this is that the ego yak-yak discounts everything, true or not, because among other things, it must have proof that something is true. The trail of substantiation, if not present to it, becomes a point of dramatic, traumatic, objection and rejection and sometimes, massive stress. So my first job in testing this idea was to calm down and set aside that loud objecting voice. It can be pretty strong and hard to ignore. What I did, my strategy if you will, was to just note and keep an incoming new thought in the background until the ego had its say and started to calm down. The new thought, sort of sitting there on the sidelines, patiently waiting, became less of a threat with time. We are not talking much time here, usually a very few minutes, before it was somewhat OK to invite that thought back to the front of my mind. From there I could consider it, explore what it might mean and gently put it forward as candidate for genuine possibility, as "the answer" or at least "an answer" or "a part answer" to the question.

To complicate this process, I found that an intuitive hit from Divine was sometimes only part of an answer. I needed to keep that one thought present and watch for part two and so on until the aha became clear. The idea of "Ask and you shall receive," paired with "Seek and ye shall find," although we have all heard these before, was the answer to the question I had just posed. I asked for Guidance and "Seek and you shall find" became evident to me. I had never experienced "Seek (ask) and you shall find" before then. I had heard it but didn't know anything about what it might really mean. But when I got it, I really got it. Then the pieces floating around began to make sense. Why? Because I was then allowing them to be sensible, at least candidates for sensible, answers. That opened the big doors. I had found an access point to the Divine labyrinth. Wow.

I note that it was that "allowing" part that brought me across the goal line on this. And I now recall times when that was the last step needed and I simply did not know it. So, revelation, if I may call it that, was on my doorstep, gently whispering and I was oblivious. Kind of sad, huh. Yet part of the discovery process. Takes time and willingness to "what if" my way along. That has worked and continues to work. I am happy.

One interesting and cool thing about these revelations is that I don't forget them. What occurred spiritually in the hospital, while I was unable to write, no one to do it for me, etc., I still remembered weeks later when I finally could type or write. It seems that the really spot-on bull's-eye messages become indelible. Isn't that a great plus?

On the fourteenth day of my stay at the hospital, I was moved from the intensive care unit, breathing on my own. The dream with the numbers on the bales now meant a lot more to me. What was going to happen on the seventeenth day and the nineteenth?

UP FROM PARALYSIS

I felt sure now that the blinking twenty-eight was telling me the day I would be going home. How could I keep from singing? There was a certain doctor that I needed to visit to debunk his story of four or five months. Bah! His comments may have been well-intentioned, but they attacked my hope; not good.

From: Barb Seiler
Sent: Wednesday, April 12, 2000 9:13 AM
To: list
Subject: Update Joe

More good news. Yesterday at 5:00 p.m. Joe was transferred from the ICU to IMCU - Intermediate Care Unit on 6B - same hospital. He came off the respirator on Monday and did well, with just oxygen assistance and so they thought to transfer him to neurology. The neurology people were a little uncomfortable with that because he still needs to be suctioned a lot for his lungs, so he went to IMCU instead. He still does need attentive care. They have 1 nurse for every 2 patients.

It was quite traumatic (no pun intended) leaving the ICU - after all, we've been bonding with those nurses for almost two weeks now - and they are lovely, lovely people. They all want Joe to come back – walking – to say goodbye when he leaves the hospital.

Visitors are still restricted and no flowers allowed yet.

His spirits are good, but I'm sure the days are long for him. The process is slow, but everyday we see more movement and slowly he is starting to lift his arms and legs, not too much, but some. His arms are the weakest still. Not sure how long he will be in IMCU, and then I suspect he will eventually make it to the neurology ward. And then he will likely be transferred to a general ward. He can't go to a general ward until he can push a call button.

Thanks to you all for being there.

Barb

Actually, I used to sing a little line from a kids' Sunday school song when I would notice a bit of progress or realize how fortunate I had been through this thing. It was "Oh, the Lord is good to me," which I think must have come from my pre-teen years somewhere. You might have heard me render this little ditty from time to time if I didn't know you were there. Then I would chuckle at the silliness and the beauty of it. More entertainment.

I often had problems with extreme irritation in my eyes. It seemed that with all the sweating and tears that my eyes would, from time to time, get filled with a toxic combination of some kind of irritating chemistry and only a thorough wash with saline would settle it down. The eyes were really sensitive and the usual drop or two of what they normally use did nothing at all. When I could only communicate with eye movement it was a tremendous challenge to "tell" the nurses that I needed my eyes washed.

The comment about the days being long for me is interesting. Some days were agonizingly long, when I would focus on "getting something," whether it be a nurse's attention or what-have-you. When I was in my own little world seeking answers and exploring how it all works, time flew by. I was infatuated by these new discoveries. And I had this corporeal entity to work through and it had experienced a severe body slam. Fatigue and inconveniences like creased sheets, etc., had to have their air time in my mind too.

The not knowing was stressful. I was so intent on "getting out" that any little thing tipped me over. Yet, somehow I was cheerful, mostly cheerful. Often, within myself, when I would forget the images and feelings of being in that sea, I was terribly lonely. Mind awake on steroids, barely able to communicate, nothing to do but count breaths or imagine a better time to come; that was me in my body. Though I was feeling quite "responsible" for keeping others encouraged I was not that great at keeping myself that way all of the time. I was certainly optimistic, though still scared. I didn't know what to expect, just that something was going to happen on the seventeenth, nineteenth and probably the twenty-eighth (or maybe the twenty-seventh) day. That part I was quite certain of and it fed me, sustained me in an unexplainable way. Those thoughts were amazingly peace-filled. It was like knowing I was getting a fabulous present but didn't yet know what that present would be. How many more sleeps?

HOW IS IT THAT WE CAN "KNOW" SOMETHING

How is it that we can "know" something with such certainty and not be able to explain what it is to another person? This kind of knowing is available, I have learned, when I get quiet and go looking, get listening. That "Seek and ye shall find" thing.

How?

1. Calm myself

2. Defocus from the world around me

3. Pose the question in a respectful asking way (I am ready to learn X and wish to receive Guidance, to see, recognize and understand the next thing that I need to know about X)

4. Stay; stay tuned into the space of the question, stay curious about any and all images that may swirl around in my mind

5. Release judgment about an answer being good enough or as expected or direct, though many times the answer is just plain blunt

6. Collect pieces of information and let those pieces appear to be unrelated if that be the case

7. Be ready to be surprised

8. Smile and say thank you

9. "Know" the answer will come

I recall using this sequence to ask for Guidance about what to say to another person who needed help (not while I was in the hospital, but in my ordinary life). I went to sleep with the "ask" delivered from my mind as I drifted into sleep. I awoke to interim answers throughout the night. There were two very clear answers delivered, or more accurately, two versions of the same answer were delivered. But they didn't "feel good," felt harsh somehow. I call them the first and second draft and they were too blunt, in my opinion. So I asked again. By morning I had version three and it felt on the bull's-eye. Strong medicine, true, the answer that was needed, simply stated. I wrote it out longhand, asked permission to deliver. Permission was granted, so handed it over and detached. I felt good about it. I don't think I could have come up with what I needed without Guidance. Maybe I could have stumbled into the first blunt version, but that third version was so much better and was a clear upgrade to what I might have expected from myself. Big plus about it all is that I detached after delivery. The old way had me standing there demanding you agree and insisting you do what I said. Euch.

The book billboards

When I returned from the hospital after my second GBS experience in 2013 and asked what to do next it was a billboard, well many billboards, all showing simply "book" hand-written large. So here I am writing this book, some writing every day. And when I don't write, the billboards come back. Relentless these messages from the other side. I love it.

Another thing that keeps on happening is that I find myself discovering insights in reading that I find lying around, whether it be news or a novel or a sign downtown or menu or instructions on how to use a new glue. All kinds of "hits," little tugs in a direction that help me write with ease. The idea that my writing has to be somehow "good" or better, that just does not seem to come up. Write, that is the invitation, so I trust that it means I have something that needs to be written and never mind the Nobel Prize in Literature.

At this point I don't even know how or by whom it will be published, though I do have a sense that it will indeed be published. This feels like the "collect information" stage. The idea of receiving information other than from the FedEx gal with a return address of the Library of All Information in the World has gone away from me. The information just shows up, and my job is to simply do that other step of "be ready to be surprised." The strangest little tidbits seem to float into my mind. I just keep them around for a while and sure enough another and then another tidbit combine to make a point for me, something worth writing that could be helpful to a reader.

This is quite empowering, as it releases me from insisting that every human on the planet fall in love with my book. It even releases me from insisting that every person who reads it must understand and/or accept every little part of my message. Not needed at all. That would be like insisting that everyone on the planet agree, on anything. Not going to happen and a fool's errand to try and make it happen. We need to let things be as they are and never mind trying to have every snowflake and daisy be identical.

I wish I could claim some ancient wisdom uncovered in a thousand-year-old container found in some remote place. It might also be really cool to call this a "secret never before revealed." Nope. I have come to believe these few things by experimenting and seeking a way to connect to Guidance. When we seek, we find. There, I mean here, a hit, just came to me. The path is "Seek and ye shall find" – again. Too easy? Too familiar? Too plain? Too sad that we have a tough time believing that. The ego wants something grande and has a tendency to discount seeking with the intuition as well as with the five senses. Intuitive seeking is not taught much, at least I don't recall a Seeking 101 class in any of my education experiences. Yet intuition rules as far as I can tell; certainly it does when looking "within."

Here is another hit, hot off the sensing – until I get hungry for a knowledge of the kind that is not yet taught, for ways to connect with Divine, to enter the flow of the subconscious, to experience direct "knowing," I won't notice it. When we want it enough we open to finding it in this strange place which we could simply call "inside of us." That is where this "knowing" resides – inside of us. Even though the access to all of this knowing is inside of us, we easily shut the door, denying ourselves that knowledge. The good news on the flip side of that coin is that we can also very easily open the door. Whether we open or close that door for ourselves is a personal choice.

Might this be an example of that free will idea that many have a tough time explaining?

Discovering Divine

I have discovered that we are an expression of the Divine. If we came from an oak tree, might it not be probable that we are some kind of oak?

A hologram is a type of image. There was a time when Visa credit cards had a holographic image of a dove etched onto them. The image, if illuminated by the right combination of pure light, as available from a laser which produces a single wavelength, tightly focused, slice of the light spectrum, that kind of pure illumination produces a three dimensional image of the etched image. The image appears in full detail and one can walk around it and see every side as if the actual physical 3D item were right there in front of us.

That alone is very cool. What is even more amazing is that if someone took that etched image and cut it up into a billion pieces one can take any of the tiny slices and illuminate it with that same pure light and the full image of the original item is reproduced in three dimensions, as if the entire original were still being used. Nothing missing.

Here is the "what if" I want you to consider very seriously. What if, you, and I, and every other person, are in fact slices of the Divine "hologram"?

What might that mean? To me it means that if I look at you, illuminate you, with pure light, could be love, I might see the Divine in you. What I see is not a part of the Divine. I see all of Divine in you. I see all of Divine in all beings. The toughest one to see Divine in, is me. Am still working on that one.

If we came from an oak tree might it not be probable that we are some kind of oak? If we came from Divine might it not be probable that we are some kind of Divine too? And the only thing in the way is how we choose to illuminate each other and what we look for. If you believe that I am a jerk, you will find all kinds of proof that I am a jerk. No matter what I do, in your mind, I am a jerk and the evidence just keeps piling up. What if, yes, what if, I believe that people are a slice of the Divine hologram and what if I choose to illuminate others with pure light and with the intention of recognizing the Divine in others? What would change for me and if you did it too what might change for you?

What if you could see yourself as a slice of the Divine hologram and if you could see yourself with the pure light of love, you would see the Divine in you, the Divine that has always been there? Me too.

What if?

The very idea of being a slice of the Divine hologram is a huge leap from conventional thinking. It means that Rumi, in his poem near the front of this book, would be right.

The Universe is not outside of you.
Look inside yourself;
Everything that you want,
You already are.

Rumi

It would mean that I am neither better nor less than you and vice versa. It would mean the end of jockeying to be "ahead," of competing for favors and of fighting and war and all of the cousins to those ideas. This concept is offered because I believe it is so. Again, I did not "find" this somewhere exotic. I found it inside of me. I remember that it is true.

From: Barb Seiler
Sent: Thursday, April 13, 2000 8:25 AM
To: list
Subject: Update Joe

Just a little more good news. When I saw Joe yesterday (after I sent the email), he had improved remarkably overnight. He can now pull his knees up and roll over. This is great as it helps relieve the pain in his back, which has been a major problem for him since he went into the hospital - probably from inactivity.

His sense of humor shone through yesterday, too. We were chatting about when he might leave intermediate care.

Joe: "Oh, probably Friday or Monday." (lip talk)

Barb: "Oh, really. I hadn't heard anything about that. No one [doctor or nurse] has said anything about that to me."

Joe: "I know. I haven't told them yet!"

He's a riot, all right!

Barb

Now that it was official that I was on the mend and on my own, there was no stopping the daily progression of returned function. I actually rolled over onto my side and could sleep in the fetal position as I normally did at home. Life was pretty good. And it got way better real fast too because now I was allowed visitors and flowers and all that other stuff. The emails and cards had sustained me and touched me so deeply while in the ICU, but there is something about seeing someone in person that cannot be captured in writing. Thank you, thank you, thank you, to all who visited. There was never a day that someone did not come to encourage me. And the amazing thing is who showed up. I mean people I could never, ever have predicted would come to visit, did so. I am so blessed!

So I was in transition. The "disease" was gone or had stopped attacking or whatever it is that diseases do after the damage. For me, now, thirteen years later, I posit that the lesson I was to learn, the insight I needed next in my life had been delivered and I had received as strong a dose of "learning" as I could absorb at the time. As I recall, this was all the remembering kind of learning. This was a time of a kind of awe about what had happened. Here I was coming out of paralysis, a string of ultra-vivid dreams, insights I could never have predicted, and I was just there, being immersed in all of that.

My message? Slow down, be more patient, easy does it, let Guidance be heard. More than that, let it be heard and followed. This is a serious upgrade. To trust Guidance enough to act upon it, is that smart? Or is it a recipe for disaster? New territory for me.

But it was not about slowing my pace of life, it was about slowing and calming and going easy on the demands I was placing on myself. I mean look at the lengths I was going to in order to save and protect others and all of this while I was the one who was paralyzed. Sheesh. Who am I to be everyone else's savior. Talk about arrogant, huh. I love the way Louise Hay says it: "If I am guided by the Divine, then who am I to 'fix' someone else? Are we not all guided? Did Divine forget someone? Do I know better than Divine?" Love it.

I somewhat absorbed the message and became more gentle with myself, but not, it seems, gentle enough, so, in 2013, kablamm, another round of GBS. Writing now, from the other side of GBS2, I feel absolutely, serenely, calm by comparison to any time that I can recall from my entire life. Guess I am getting it more this time and I no longer wonder if I have gotten it this time. I believe I have and part of the evidence is that I am smiling at myself as the olde triggers show up and they just pass me by. No not all of them. But a huge percentage of the past triggers are just not triggers any more, they are memories that I can smile at, even chuckle at, sometimes laugh out loud.

"Life is good, the world is round," as Mom came to say when she was over eighty. I guess that means evolution is real since I am understanding that and living it at age sixty-two, an improvement of eighteen years.

Dare I say? Dare I say that I feel like I have been sprinkled with fairy dust and now "see differently"? Yuh, I am saying that. I feel just so much more OK with, well, with everything. What used to bug me to distraction, doesn't anymore. What else is there to say?

Want this too? My best spidey sense says, for me, "choose to be OK with all that bugs me" as the big answer "from the other side." No, I can't pretend it is easy since it took me two bouts of GBS, paralysis big-time, to come to this place of soft calm and clarity. That does not mean you must go through such trials. But if you are as stubborn as I can be, some call it dedicated and focused and strong and powerful and persistent and committed, those are words that described me, if you relate, well, it may take a baseball bat up the side of the head and more than once, to get you to seriously take on this new point of view. Maybe not, but that is what it took for me. I wonder what your message might be?

If we meet, please don't be disappointed that I don't sport a shiny gold halo. Sorry O, as they say in Ghana. What you may notice is that I am a pretty happy guy. I am happy when others have a tough time being happy. If you know me from the past you will notice the difference. People who knew me say, "Hey, give me a pound of what you've been smoking." I have this kind of ease around me and a simple happiness. I just feel happy. It is an infectious kind of happy.

At least from where I sit, it is just that simple.

"Choose to be OK with all that bugs me"

Forgiveness is not "it"

"**B**e OK with all that bugs me" segues to another concept that I have pondered for a few years now – forgiveness. It is touted as one of the greatest ideas ever. I used to be a big fan. Then I got to thinking and came to the question, "If I am forgiving you, what were my thoughts about you before I decided to forgive you?" Oh my, those are not nice thoughts. Judgment, labeling, accusations, anger, threats, maybe even hate. Ouch. As I noticed this bagful of thoughts, it was easy to see that it was I that I needed to forgive. I needed to forgive myself for thinking those thoughts and taking myself down-spiral into the pits of that chart from Power vs Force, into guilt and shame, the very opposite of Divine. I was making my own hell, and it felt that way too. Body chemistry producing toxic euch – stomach pain, shortness of breath, tight muscles, sleeplessness, agitation a lot of the time. It does not get much worse.

Now forgiving you, what it took to do that, came in a distant second place to what was needed to forgive me. I made the sounds of forgiving you, but no matter how many times I moaned "mea culpa" the bad feelings would not go away until I could forgive myself.

How come?

I think it is because it was I that did it to me so it had to be I who undid it for me.

How?

Now that is the million-dollar question. And what, exactly, is forgiveness, anyway? As it happens, it is not a million-dollar question at all. Since I made it up, could I not just unmake it up? Every hurt I experienced came from a thought that I fabricated. I fabricated the thought and I fabricated the idea that some thoughts were bad thoughts and I further fabricated that I ought to feel bad about it all. The moment I noticed that, I knowticed it was all a chimera, a nothing, a piece of clothing hung over a chair that turned into a boogey man when the lights were turned out. Hah! I laugh a lot about it all now.

I coined the word knowticing in my first book written in 2002, Personal Fulfillment is Success. To knowtice is to notice with the intent to find an aha, a possible learning, of some kind.

Acceptance *IS* "it"

Bonus is that I don't need to forgive you because you really didn't do anything to me. I did all of that to me. You were just living your life having your experiences. Louise Hay is so right. I am having my life and you are having yours and Divine is available to both of us, so let it unfold, and it will, and get over my self-designated holiness, whereby I arrogantly forgive you.

The upgrade to forgiveness, what would that be? If I didn't have all those thoughts (judging, labeling, accusing, etc.) that bring with them the hurt in me that I need to forgive, what thought(s) might be healthier, more true? It has taken me some years to come to the conclusion that if I simply live in Acceptance of others, forgiveness is not needed. Forgiveness is not even a poor distant relative of the Divinity of Acceptance. The Divine would never judge, at least not any Divine that I would consider worshipping.

A Course In Miracles states in Lesson 46, "God does not forgive because She/He has never condemned." And in paragraph two, "… yet, although God does not forgive, His/Her Love is nevertheless the basis of forgiveness."

How is it that a parent can interact with their newborn baby, that little bundle of puking, poop-producing and wailing infant, without judgment? Is it not because there is no expectation, no set of rules (yet) about what behavior is accepted? Is the baby Accepted? The parent decided, in their mind, that whatever the baby does it is nothing less than perfect and they Accept the child without conditions. This is love.

That changes. Sometimes way fast. The parent, in time, becomes an ever-present source of, yes, judgment, which is mixed in with the Love. This is the environment most of us grow up within, not because we have nasty parents, but because this is something that we, as a species, seem to just do, not even realizing it. Even in the Christmas carol, "… no crying He makes," is some kind of testimony to how good He is; "bad babies cry" is implied. Sheesh. We are raised in an atmosphere that has Love indeed, but mixed in is this toxic judgment that comes and goes, that confuses our understanding of what Love really is. Is it any wonder that Love is such a mystery? We have been raised in an environment of confusion about what Love is. All of us.

Bottom line? Acceptance is the real answer. Acceptance is what Louise Hay is speaking about. Acceptance is the vehicle that takes us all to happiness, bliss and Divine Guidance. Acceptance is Love. When I choose Acceptance, including, and this may not be all that easy, Acceptance of myself, forgiveness is no longer needed. Forgiveness is needed within the old paradigm of eye-for-an-eye and all that kind of thinking. Retribution is a result of forgiveness thinking.

Acceptance is not condoning or encouraging or in any way standing apart from acts of non-Love. By all means, we need to help each other experience Love through Acceptance. If we all were to act from Acceptance there would be no war or violence or hunger or prejudice or … the list is too long to include here. Until we get to that magic time I recommend that we watch for opportunities to be Loving to one another. How about saying "thank you" when you receive your next meal. If you also want to offer thanks to the Divine, yes, do that. But I mean saying thank you to the person who assembled the meal and is serving it to me, to you. What about the people we meet in our daily goings on, the coffee clerk, the colleague, the boss (they need thanks too), the children in our lives? Thank you to all. Send Acceptance to that person whose appearance really makes me nervous. On we go to a better planet to live on. I start with thank you and move ever closer to Acceptance that maybe, just maybe, that other person is having a valid Divine experience that I may not understand. Drop the judgment, etc., and the world becomes a better place.

Forgiveness has been trumped. You and I are invited to adopt this paradigm of Acceptance. Shall we?

Acceptance *IS* "it."

The speck and the plank

There is a Bible story about the speck in your neighbor's eye and the plank in your own eye. Is this not the judgment thing said large? Here I go around "fixing" other people whom I have decided need fixing, while I walk around with the equivalent of a plank sticking out of my eye. That is funny.

Rhonda Britten once wrote an article in Choice magazine about the three basic fears, one of which is fear of looking stupid. Ever experience that fear yourself? Yah, me too. When I am in that fear-of-looking-stupid-place, one of the more common reactions is to start telling everyone around me about all the things that I know. Unbidden, I start dissertation after dissertation on trivia that you are probably not interested in. If you do get a word in, I'll upstage you with an even juicier factoid. When I am afraid of looking stupid, I act, well, pretty stupid (reinforcing that looking-stupid image). Funny, just like that plank in the eye story. I get full of my self-judgment, start yakking away, turn you off, and behold, I experience that "Oh drat, did it again, I am such a _____" and am then a prime customer for some forgiveness. And I did it to me. No help needed from anyone else.

How do I find my "planks"? Most of us have a few, which get activated by certain situations. They are not necessarily visible to the person who has them. Who has enough self-esteem to ask in public to have others name their planks?

One oblique way to find hints about my planks is to notice when I generate an impact that I did not intend to generate. Even the oblivious person, yakking ad infinitum, eventually gets the feeling that folks are not wanting to listen to them. If I can catch myself having that feeling and separate it from the actions that are bringing it to me, the yakking, then I may be able to conclude, "When I yak-yak-yak, folks don't want to listen to me." From there, the possibility of seeing the plank in my eye arises, that I so fear looking stupid, that I overcompensate by yakking ad infinitum and thus come off looking stupid. Bingo. I now have an understanding that brings me to a place of choosing better for myself. Gotta notice that disquiet and pull back a bit to observe it all in play. And then laugh.

1. Notice disquiet

2. Pull back to Observer position (judgment-free, just observing)

3. Without judgment, name what I see

4. Play "what if," i.e., what if that is true or not true or whatever...

5. Choose different behavior next time

6. Let myself laugh with me and about me

Rising Above the Room

I started to have a dreamlike vision from time to time. It would happen when a patient close by was experiencing great pain. I would see myself above the landscape where the arbor was, on a cloud-like plain. I was a sort of cartoon character with my profile facing to the left and my hair (lots of it) blowing to the left (yeah, backwards). There was often another person there on my right and he had a Clint Eastwood style of hat on. His face was not clear to me. Probably my Guide, as before. I was calling to the other patient and inviting them to join us here "above" where there was no pain. Sometimes they did and it seemed to lessen their distress and sometimes not. This probably happened about half a dozen times over the next few days. I can revisit it now with no effort at all. It seems that we can get to a place where pain is at least subdued.

From: Barb Seiler
Sent: Thursday, April 13, 2000 6:16 PM
To: list
Subject: Update Joe

Yes!! He talks. Visitors - yes! Flowers - Yes!

At 4:45 p.m. today Joe was transferred to 3B - Centennial Building -

Victoria General. (Room 3154, I think). He would welcome visitors,

starting tomorrow.

At 3:30 p.m. this afternoon Joe was "corked." That is to say, they put a cork in his trachea and he now talks. He was talking on his own somewhat, a low raspy whisper, but it took a lot of effort. Now he speaks normally just like he used to. The only drawback is that his oxygen levels still need to be assisted and therefore he has an oxygen mask - which he doesn't like much. The good news is that they expect to take the trachea [tube] out completely tomorrow if he does well overnight and he appears to be doing so. He is eating a liquid diet, through a straw, but they're hoping to put him on solid food, once the trachea is out. Tomorrow seems to be the big day.

Barb

I had a rather tough night with a huge case of indigestion. Since I had eaten nothing in weeks, the source was a mystery. At 4:30 a.m. the Resident visited and gave me a huge dose of morphine after telling me that it is not uncommon to have patients who have been on a respirator for a while to develop a stomach ulcer. Great! I slept until nearly 7:30 and they gave me another shot and I slept until about 9:00 a.m. Ahhhhhhh, the stomach pressure was finally gone. They started including an antacid in my daily pills.

Day 17, Trachea Tube Removed

From: Barb Seiler
Sent: Thursday, April 14, 2000 7:18 PM
To: list
Subject: Joe Update

Joe had his trachea [tube] out today and he was pleased – just two more tubes to go.

He was transferred again to Floor 4B (General Medicine), room 086.

Barb

It is the seventeenth day, and my trachea tube is removed. The dream with the numbers is proving to provide valuable information. I wonder what will happen on the nineteenth day?

The tube was removed at 4:35 p.m. and supper arrived at about 5:10. I was fed a piece of boiled potato with butter on it. I can still taste it. Glorious! My taste buds were extremely sensitive. I was tasting in Technicolor and surround sound. Wonderful!

I was allowed to see visitors that day too. Boy, what a wonderful day!

Today, nearly thirteen years later, I can still taste that potato with butter. An IMAX taste sensation for sure. Such a small thing. Or was it? I was, in the minds of many, back from the brink. I knew what that "brink" was like, it was in the well with "submit" rolling past on that screen. I was, I believe, given the choice to stay or to withdraw from the earthly experience I am having. Some say that we are provided three exit opportunities. That was definitely one of them, in my opinion. The taste of that potato reminded me of earthly delights, experiences that I was not appreciating. Since then I more often pause to notice the experiences of earth. Food has more taste and subtle spices are now both noticed and appreciated. I cook more and experiment with spices, like trying, say, thyme in my vegetable soup, just to figure out what that spice can bring. Fun.

Life as delight

This is actually a pretty cool way to experience life. By "this" I mean being delighted more often. Seems to me that the doorway to being more delighted with what I had been ignoring before was opened wider. Do I now feel rapture in every moment with every thing? Nope, not that fancy. But I do find myself more often pausing to notice all manner of (before) trivial things. More than that, I sometimes find myself looking for the new knowing in whatever it is that I am noticing. What is it about "this" that I seem to be noticing and that has my attention? What is here for me? What is the knowticing in "this"?

The trick seems to be not to take it all too seriously. When I get all serious about finding a big hit from a noticing, it spoils the experience and gets very tense. Small, at least in the measurement norms of many people, is actually just fine. They add up. The bigger ahas come before I know it. The small noticings, I mean knowticings, I just keep to myself and do my best to put them into the library in my mind and just let them sit there until they either mature and morph into an aha by themselves or get combined with other noticings to make the next knowticing. Some are just not anything that I recognize. Oh well.

An essential ingredient in this process is to "allow" the small hits to be as important as any other. Size is not the issue. A hard concept when we consider the worldly penchant for measures of most things. The other essential ingredient is to "collect evidence." When an aha starts to form I cast my awareness around to see what will support or undo that beginning aha. If neither, what has worked best for me is to do nothing and just smile at that internal yakky voice that really hates that option. Yakky wants me to get animated about it all. When I manage to bypass that option, life is better. That's my formula for becoming more self-aware, more clear on what it all means. If there is something to it, fine; if not, fine as well, go for the bypass.

1. Allow small hits

2. Collect evidence

3. Let "no hit this time" be OK; just shrug, doing nothing is fine

4. Laugh at the internal voice that has such a tough time with stuff like this

One more important noticing. I notice that if I am to pay attention and I'm not doing so, the message comes back. I saw a license plate the other day with a number and the initials of one of our daughters on it. I smiled and thought isn't that nice, then carried on my merry way. Though I did not see that license plate again the image of it kept popping into my awareness. Not just a few times but many times over the next days. Finally, I looked up the number in a book that claims to explain such noticings as Angel messages. Sure enough, the message for the number was to continue seeking and following messages that come into my awareness. I was in the midst of the book-writing experience and was seeking Guidance constantly. I was feeling a bit sluggish and boom, in comes this message of encouragement. How cool is that? I felt energized again. Go!

And I am smiling.

Yah know, this might be a lot of woo woo or it might not be the real thing. Or it could be real. For me, it is giving me insight and confidence and happiness so I really don't mind which it is. It is working well for me and it is working so well that I invite you to try it too. Let the layer of messages of knowing below the thoughts we call waking thoughts, the subconscious stuff, let those percolate up. Some may remember the old-fashioned percolator for making coffee. Put in the water and the basket with the coffee, place the lid on tight, plug it in and watch the little glass ball on top of the lid. Even though the pot is plugged in and "working" there is not even one bubble seen in that glass ball for quite some time. But soon enough, might be minutes, glub, one bubble. Then glub glub, a few bubbles and before you know it, glub, glub, glub it goes. Even then the coffee is not yet ready. We need to let that bubbling action work for a while before good coffee is ready to enjoy.

Let your process of coming to knowticing be like that percolator. Patience and certainty that it will come, these are the recommended ingredients. Oh, and laugh a lot at what may come up while you wait because seriousness will trample knowticing almost every time. That delight thing.

Isn't this just that "Seek and ye shall find" thing again? If I am not interested in coffee, that percolator won't even be taken out of the cupboard, let alone be loaded and plugged in and watched with interest and positive curiosity and anticipation. It all goes together. When I seek, finding becomes more likely.

One more very important thing. If a person does this they are not better, holier, in any way "above" a person who does not do it. I have this idea that I am to write this stuff down, from my place of truth (from my own knowticings) and I'm done at that point.

THE LAST TUBES

My objectives were to now rid myself of the remaining tubes; a feed tube, catheter and IV. The feed tube could go if I could hold down the solid food that was now available to me. The catheter could go if I could handle the urine bottle myself. The IV was needed at least until the last antibiotic dosage and the double dose of immunoglobulin was installed, both scheduled to happen on Monday.

So I got to work on the urine bottle. I could not reliably grab it unless it was placed just so on the side table and the table placed just so beside the bed. Well, the nurses didn't need to know about those restrictions. I was able to demonstrate handling of the bottle on Monday and convinced them to get rid of the catheter. Good.

Well, mostly good. Before the removal a nurse came in to change my pajamas. She yanked on the bottoms without noticing that the prior nurse had slipped the catheter tube into the slot in the front that usually has a zipper in street pants. Nearly lost my penis before she noticed my, uhm, discomfort at her pulling.

Holding down solid food was no problem at all so the food tube also went first thing Monday, when the doctor came for rounds.

That left the IV. The doctor said that once the immunoglobulin and antibiotics were in me that it could go too. There were fourteen bottles of immunoglobulin and one bag of antibiotics to install. At about 1:30 in the morning (Tuesday) it was finally done. Out with the tubes, at last. It was April 18, the twenty-first day.

I missed the event predicted to occur on the nineteenth day. It may have been in another place and I will learn about it later. I do not know.

I guess I didn't need to know. This idea of needing to know, where does that come from? In my experience, both by observing myself and the many coaching clients I have worked with, it is the ego that gets jittery when it does not know something. Makes that bit of information into a dramatic trauma, a thing to fear, a growing list of disastrous possibilities, all imaginary, none have happened and very few are realistically likely to happen. One thing I am learning is to laugh a lot at that nervous little voice. I have come to notice when I get jittery about a future possibility, it shows up as tension in the shoulders. That flag tells me to do a mental check on the reality of the supposed threat and in the majority of cases, no, there is not a lion in the backseat of the car nor an alligator under the desk, no real threat of any kind anywhere. So I get to smile, even laugh sometimes and short-circuit the false fear. Makes my life a lot more pleasant. People often comment on the calm state that I seem to carry around with me. Infectious stuff. Just as a fear-filled person brings tension into the room, a calm person can bring ease and trust and smiles into the room. Not knowing used to be a big stressor. Not so much anymore.

My focus now centered on getting out of bed. I could not yet sit up because I got too dizzy. I would use the electric bed controls to raise my upper body as high as I could stand and try to stay there for at least twenty minutes per hour. I started at about five minutes and worked my way up. Amazingly this little thing was work and I found myself exhausted as I moved the bed back down.

It was and remains, interesting how focused I can get. All that talk of noticing and knowticing, gone. I had a job to do and it was on my critical path to the exit from the hospital. I was on it big-time. I also recall how time almost didn't exist in the usual form. I was into my self-designed exercise and routines. I believed these were the right plan and was not to be dissuaded. Isn't this a beautiful aspect of being human? We can, I certainly can, get absorbed and lose track of time when consumed with something decided to be oh, so important. Sort of like clawing my way back to the surface after being dumped into a deep ocean. It is life and death combined. All of it made up. Exhilarating! And why not? The same kind of energy is available to propel me, or you, to a great discovery. Edison and Einstein and many others entered this kind of deep focus state to find their "answers." They had questions that needed answering and results that needed to be accomplished. Me too! A time when all that stubborn resolve paid dividends.

What I am saying here is that to stay in knowticing mode is not some sort of badge of honor. The human ways are for us to experience, so let's do that too.

Invitations from the "other side"

M akes me wonder what might happen if I applied that level of focus and effort and dedication to a few more things that cross my mind in life. Those little "what if" thoughts, what are those? An invitation from "the other side"? OK, so what if they are invitations? Ohhh, that is intriguing. This feels like a hit, right here, right now. "Hey Joseph, 'what if' those little thoughts, the ones that seem at least a little bit intriguing, what if they are invitations from the other side?"

Wow.

Invitations from the "other side"? Are we not getting out of bounds here? I think not. The "other side" is gently whispering to me all the time. If I don't hear it, or even if I do hear it, if I don't act on it, the message repeats until I do hear. There are many reports of people having this kind of gentle whisper experience and have it follow them around until they did what they needed to do. Where we get creeped out is the idea that this whisper is sinister and not on our side, that it can and will hurt us. Sorry folks. Not true. This is soul/Spirit speaking, not ego, not even heart. Soul. *Wait, being smitten with love is heart. So, OK, could be heart. Back to the Soul.* And it is not stalking us but rather patiently waiting until we are ready to hear it. Ever had that "gee, I should have done this a long time ago" feeling of relief? Yeah, me too. Now I know why it felt like joyous relief instead of the feeling of getting a nag to leave me alone.

Soul is not afraid, cannot be hurt, sees across all time and has only love to fuel it. How could soul be sinister? It can't.

What I need to do is to get into the habit of listening for the messages from the Soul. Some will call it the Universal subconscious mind, some say it is Angels, some say it is woo woo and we really ought to get over ourselves. One thing that I am finding really helpful in this kind of endeavor is to practice stopping and listening, but do it without demanding it be a certain way. Approach with beginner's mind, not knowing and curious. Stopping seems to be key.

1. Stop

2. Ask "what is next or what do I need to know or what am I missing or..."

3. Ask, invite and open myself to receiving (whatever that is for you)

4. Listen (with my spidey sense)

5. Whatever I notice, let that be perfect, just make note of it all

6. Listen some more

7. If needed, repeat for, say, two minutes

That's it. Well, almost. I accept the insights I have collected and written down as potential messages to play "what if" with.

- What if this is true?

- What if this is a warning? (ego will want to know)

- What if this is a really smart move?

- What if…? (play)

And again, open to hearing something worthwhile. Or not…

This is a dangerous spot, this part of the process. Why? Because I can get all serious and demand some kind of six-o'clock-news-worthy aha. **That is the least likely possibility of what will show up.** When I suggest listening for something worthwhile I mean something that may tug or seem odd or feel familiar, something that I notice in any way. I look at my desktop and my eyes come to a piece of paper with a quote on it. That paper has been there for years because the quote on it is a favorite. How is it that I am noticing it right now? The quote is "Fear in your mind produces fear in your life. That is the meaning of hell." Oh boy, so if I had any fear that "no one" will get this and "everyone" will think it is dumb and such, guess I am being Guided to let those ideas slide back into the useless pit they came up from. Nice.

Use the process. Ask, listen and be open to receive. Guidance is always available and the only weird thing is that we humans seem to have developed the hurtful habit of ignoring it.

The visitors were a wonderful support. Each day someone different and so many surprises, people I could never expect to visit did so and it was truly wonderful. It was rare that more than one person was there at the same time. This made it especially nice as I could give attention to each of them. Barb was there every day, usually a few hours in the morning and then again in the late afternoon. Leslie became my supper partner and would feed me because I could not yet control the utensils or lift the food high enough to get into my mouth. Food was wonderful. Tasty and a good variety. I was told that if I liked the food so much they would use that as testimony that I was not ready to go home yet.

It was around this time that Barb had told me that she was going to be in to visit the next day after going to the gym, which meant about 9 a.m., but she became involved in errands and didn't come to the hospital until after 11 a.m. I was totally undone and in tears when she arrived. I had thought the worst, that she had been in a car accident or something like that. Who would support Leslie? What about the other children (young adults)? Who would take care of the dog? How could I do anything about it, since I couldn't even feed myself yet? My stay in the hospital found me highly sensitive to emotional outpouring and this day demonstrated just how close to the surface my emotions were.

This event also showed me how much I relied on others for, well, everything. My self-absorption about getting out of the hospital drew me into a state where I was in my own world of "the next task/accomplishment/goal." That was my conscious life. As I now reflect on that, I see so many years of that type of behavior as dominant in my past. See some of it now too, but not nearly as often. Not to say that deep and enduring focus is "bad" or otherwise, but I do conclude that it is surprisingly common even though, I dare say, not always in the best interests of the one doing it.

Imagine that we are particles in some kind of cosmic soup (which I believe we are) and that in this soup we are all floating around together. It is like when a group of us is close together and someone starts to giggle. Before you know it we are joining in. When one of us gets agitated, we all feel it. So when I am self-absorbed and bearing down on accomplishing some goal or other, I, to some extent, insulate myself from the giggles and from the agitation of others nearby. I can also infect their mood. I can feed isolation by feeling isolated. By nearby I mean "close" in the sense of people who can have an effect on me because of my particular connection to them. That could be a stranger who is physically very near or a loved one thousands of miles away. If I maintain this insulated state for long periods I miss the giggles and the agitation, positive or negative, of the world around me. People may start to forget to include me in their lives because I am just not showing much interest, I don't connect. One day I come out of my deep focus and find myself rather alone. Just noticing that now. Nothing new here, but it has my attention at the moment. I don't much like being alone. I sometimes too much like getting the job done.

Hmmm? Whom do I need to show some presence to right now? I mean, to whom do I need to be more present now, right now? To whom do you? (After writing this, I began to phone people I hadn't connected with in months. That was fantastic.)

On April 18 I was to sit in the ordinary chair (unlike the special one I sat in while in the ICU) beside the bed for the first time. I had been practicing as best I could by raising the bed. The physio people sat me on the side of the bed and I just could not get rid of the dizziness and the sweat was pouring off of my brow. We had to abandon the attempt. I was very disappointed and became depressed for the first time since entering the recovery stage. I was afraid that this meant something bad and that I may not get up for a long time. It was difficult.

April 19 was a much better day. I actually stood for nearly two minutes and then sat in the chair for over twenty minutes. My confidence soared. There was no stopping me now.

Ahh, the number 19, is this it? Just seeing this possibility now, in 2013. Cool. That tricky Guidance that does not speak English can switch the decoder without telling me. This may well be the whole story. Fun whether it is or it isn't.

The dream, or image, of being above the land where the fiery arbor stood, would arise from time to time when I would hear a patient in severe pain or would hear about someone else that I knew who was somewhere else in the hospital. It seemed to just arise on its own from time to time. The image of the arbor was now very far away although still a distinct item on the landscape below me, where my robed self still stood. The sky was no longer dark and seemed to have weather with some days being clear and some cloudy, but always light.

From: Barb Seiler
Sent: Thursday, April 20, 2000 11:36 AM
To: list
Subject: Progress Report – Joe

As you know Joe has been in the General Medicine ward since last Thursday.

A few days after he was there, the last of his tubes were removed. That was a relief. Physio comes around daily and a few days ago, they had him standing – assisted, of course, by the side of the bed for about 2 minutes. He does this everyday, now. Yesterday, he sat in a chair (assisted into it) for about one and a half hours. At first sitting up made him a little dizzy but that seems to have passed.

There is talk that today the physio people may try him on the walker. He is determined to get home as soon as possible. He has made a tentative "deal" with the doctor – ever the negotiator! – that if he can get out of bed, walk to the bathroom, manage in there, and walk back and get into bed that maybe, just maybe, he can come home next week sometime.

He still does not have complete use of his hands. We still assist him with eating, but we did play some cards during the last two days. We started with crib – he only has to hold 6 cards – he won twice! Yesterday, we advanced to two-handed whist – where he had to hold 13 cards. He can organize the cards, take one from his hand, but I put it on the table for him, and gather the tricks, as well as deal for him. But everyday something else improves. The medical staff say he is progressing quickly, compared to most cases. Yesterday, he was able to lift himself from a lying to a sitting position (in the bed, without the bed coming up, too). He doesn't sit up for long, as it is very energy sapping but he gets there, and gets back lying down.

Rehab is coming to see him today, but it will be a question of an available bed, Apparently there is a two-three week waiting list. By that time he'll likely be home, but we'll see what they say.

All this considered, we are grateful for the blessings we have, including good and caring family and friends.

I'll let you know when he "gets out"!

Barb

Today I walked into the hallway, and back, using a high arm support walker. Big smile. My sense is that if I walk then I can get out of here and once mobile that all the other functions can be developed after. I shaved myself today too. It was not fancy. The hardest part was to press the button on the shaving gel can. I used both hands to do that while pressing the can into my thigh. Then I used both hands to hold the razor while I moved my head to accomplish the shave. It felt good to get that little bit of independence back; to be able to do something myself again.

I became concerned about being left in the hospital over the coming Easter weekend without enough help to get me up into the walker. If that happened I would (I thought) languish (or rot, from my point of view) through the long four-day holiday. So I lobbied hard to get the nurses to help me up into the walker twice today hoping it would be enough to allow me to do it myself after that and solve the weekend fear. I also negotiated with the doctor about my going home. They agreed (see email). Now I was, again, one very focused fellow.

Friday was walk day for me. I would go every two hours and wanted to make a loop around one section of the ward that would be about 200 meters. In the middle of the day they needed a high walker for someone else, so I traded for a low walker with the support rail height approximately at my waist. It was tricky for a bit, but by the end of the day I was beyond my distance objective and was contemplating a few steps without a walker. That would have to wait until tomorrow.

Saturday was more of the same, progress mixed, as always, with a wonderful group of caring visitors. By the end of the day I decided to park the walker in the hallway as some sort of declaration that I could walk to and from my bed without it. I was very happy. I also managed to get to the bathroom without the walker. I was home free. All I had to do now was to wait out the Easter weekend until the doctor returned to release me. I expected that to be Tuesday (the twenty-eighth day) because Easter Monday was also a holiday.

April 23 was Easter Sunday. Life is a beach. I was ready to do my demonstration for the doctor. What could be better? And Leslie was the Easter Bunny this year, bringing me the usual chocolate treats.

<pre>
From: Barb Seiler
Sent: Monday, April 24, 2000 10:33 AM
To: list
Subject: Good News – Joe
</pre>

Joe has met his goal of being able to get out of bed, walk to the bathroom, and back to bed without, yes, without a walker. That man is determined to come home on Tuesday!

He spent the weekend walking the halls of the hospital, 3-4 times a day and graduated from the tall walker to the waist high one. Yesterday when we went in to visit he had positioned his walker in the hall, almost like a sign that he didn't really need it. And he probably doesn't. He doesn't move very fast, mind you, but he gets there – and if he started to tip over, he still hadn't the full upper body strength to pull himself upright, but everyday there is some marked improvement in what he can do. He's not that good at crib or scrabble, though, I keep beating him! (He gives me a run for my money, though)

He plans to get dressed on Tuesday morning, and be sitting on the side of the bed, when the doctor comes in, so he can then demonstrate that he kept his part of the bargain – and thus the doctor should keep his and sign the discharge papers. This is dependent on the approval from the physio people as well. They have to believe it is safe for him to go home.

Anyway, I'll let you know if he "gets out" on Tuesday.

Barb

Monday brought the unexpected. The doctor was in, even though it was a holiday! And I would not allow them to renege on their side of the bargain. I weighed myself that morning and was twenty pounds down from normal. I smelled exactly like someone who had not showered or bathed in a tub for twenty-seven days. It was time to go and I left the hospital walking unaided. The ICU nurses had asked me to stop by the day I was released. I did that gladly. They had been very good to me. As I entered the ICU they began to applaud and I almost fell down because I was overcome with emotion and gratitude for their kindness.

THE WONDER OF SMALL THINGS

When we got home, finally, a bath. Oh, the wonder of small things.

I thought to go for a short walk after supper. So out the front door I went. However, I had to go down the two steps to the driveway level, and my left leg let go under me pretty much as it had on March 29. I was on my back and unable to move. I called out to Barb who, shaking just a little, helped me up. I walked on the street to the closer corner and back. That was about it. I was tired already.

From: Barb Seiler
Sent: Monday, April 24, 2000 9:20 PM
To: list
Subject: Ahead of Schedule!

Joe has come home!

At 2:15 p.m. this afternoon, Joseph Henu Seiler walked, under his own steam, into the ICU to bid adieu to the nurses who so beautifully cared for him in the initial stages of his illness. They applauded as he walked in! (They had all said he was to do this before he dared leave the hospital ~!)

Joe's message to the nurses and doctors was to "please tell future patients who have GBS about his speedy recovery so that they can draw hope from that, rather than the much more pessimistic estimates that they would find in published literature. " It's all about hope, without it we are lost.

According to them and other medical staff he is the fastest recovery case they have ever seen. Are we surprised!

He is happy to be home and would welcome anyone who would like to come and visit him at home, pretty much any time of the day or evening – as he says: "it's not like I am going anywhere."

He also wants me to let you know that since he has yet to negotiate stairs, he can't yet get to his room (computer) and therefore, won't be "emailable" for a while. So if you have any message for him, please feel free to send it to me and I will share with him.

I guess our email experience is almost over. I would like to thank each and every one of you for allowing me to share Joe's progress with you. It was very helpful to me to be able to do this because it gave me a real sense of support. It allowed me to articulate and thus review in my own mind the progress he was making and gave me the hope I needed. It was so nice to know that so many people cared and the energy sent by just you being there was, I believe, very instrumental in Joe's rapid recovery. He said himself, that when everyday I had some card, or email response from someone that I read to him, that he drew strength from that.

Barb

PS – I may send an "epilog" in a little while.

As I worked my way along, it soon came time to send my own email to "the list" of wonderful supporters that Barb had been asked to keep up to date as the GBS affair unfolded.

From: Joseph Seiler
Sent: Wednesday May 3, 2000 9:49 AM
To: list
Subject: Good News – Joe

I think it is time to call this affair ended. I am now able to walk down stairs, frontwards. I walked to the Dairy Queen today (2.1 km each way) to have a banana split and intend to start the circuit (with about 10 lbs load) at the gym on Monday. I am not all the way to my usual strength (I can only just lift a two liter of milk with one hand) and won't be for a while, but to the disinterested observer I appear pretty normal.

This has certainly been an extraordinary event in my life. GBS is like a drive-by shooting, no reason. That I have come through it with such unbelievable speed is due to two factors. One is my stubborn belief that the mind does tell the body what to do and that I make my own future, doctor's predictions be damned. The other is the astonishing support that you beautiful folks provided me every single day; emails, cards, visits, gifts, phone calls, prayers and just plain olde nice thoughts. I felt it all. I am humbled by your overwhelming show of love. It did more for me than anything else. Your outpouring will never be forgotten. We are connected in some way and I am indebted for your unceasing kindness.

I plan to start normal things like meetings with clients, etc., the week of the 22nd. I expect to be on the motorcycle around then too.

Thank you so much for making my recovery possible so quickly.

Each day allowed me to go further and by May 19, one-month-plus-one day after I had first been able to stand up (two minutes only), I managed to trot the 2.6 kilometers to the gym. Is this the "19" that was in my dream? Or was it the nineteenth of April when I actually first walked? I don't know. I don't need to know.

I was measured by the neurologist on May 26 where we discovered that some muscles were still as much as 60% slower than "normal" but that most are nearly normal and all are on the mend. I will run ten miles again this year, but not this month. I can't yet do even one push-up (I used to do over forty) but will, soon enough. The body was not yet totally ready to do all that I asked of it and had received before. It needs time. I can wait and in the interim keep exercising at the gym and, as much as I am able, lead a normal life. Life is a beach.

THE PEAPOD DREAM

I reflected often on what was the reason and what was to change as a result of my GBS holiday. One dreamed image arose clearly and repeatedly. I was in a peapod drifting in a wonderful and large river with high banks on each side. The sun was shining, the temperature perfect, the drifting of the pod gentle and I saw a bend in the river ahead. I felt absolutely safe and was just "there" waiting for what is to come with calm and an easy joy that all was right with me. The fact that I was exposed in the middle of this large body of water and had no ability to control the pod and that my "ship" was not exactly of a strong material didn't seem to have any effect on my peacefulness in the scene. It could mean that I am to just "be" and not concern myself about the future. It will be provided and it will be wonderful, or so it seemed from the image (submit?) What is the reason and what is to change was not perfectly clear to me, but I did sense that a little less empire-building was probably appropriate. (I quite quickly, and to the dismay of my then partner, dissolved the one partnership that was heading towards "building" a machine) Since then a few other significant events have supported the "Relax, what you are intended to do will come soon enough" message.

So the story is ended and begun all at the same moment. I experienced Guillan-Barre Syndrome and experienced connection to a stream of messages, some of which I may never understand. I am different, hopefully better, and waiting, eagerly and gently at the same time, yet happily for the joy the future will bring. That I passed through this in only twenty-seven days, rather than the predictions of many months, is a part of the mystery of it all. I sought out the doctor that I argued with in the emergency on March 30 about his grim prediction and he was happy that he had erred. If you, or someone you know has GBS, tell them about me. Twenty-seven days is a lot easier to handle than four-months-plus.

June 4, 2000

Epilog to GBS 2000

Thus ended my experience with GBS. Except it was not the end at all. There are at least two branches that grew out of this event. The first is what I did with the "insight" I had received in those twenty-seven days in March/April 2000 and the second is the return of GBS in January of 2013.

Although I thought I understood the message from the dream experience of me in that very large river floating without steerage or power beyond my hands, in that very vulnerable peapod, I am now convinced I understood almost nothing. Or shall I say, I acted as if I understood almost nothing because so little changed in my direction in life. Yes, I had calmed somewhat and felt less driven. That much was true. However, within six months my days were almost as they had been with regard to my focus and what was important day to day.

By the Autumn I had registered to run the half marathon in the annual Kentville, Nova Scotia, Thanksgiving Harvest event. This was about proving to myself that I really was OK again. I had completed the full marathon, my first, at age forty-seven

(3:51:11) so that was a checkmark on my bucket list. This half marathon was some kind of a confirmation that the Spring GBS experience was indeed behind me. My ego needed this.

I don't recall my run completion time but do remember very clearly walking off the run a bit after completing and looking up to see the physio lady who had worked with me in the hospital. Our eyes met as she came through the finish gate. It was a moment of joyous reunion. "The physio lady!" "The GBS guy!" And a sincere hug. I guess that was the official end of my GBS experience. Had I not just completed a half marathon and had it witnessed by a hospital representative? Yes, it was officially over now.

My activity, day to day, although a touch gentler than when I was working in our company, was still go, go. I was engaged, but in building the next business, Coaching for Executives and other influencers in business. Lots of training beyond the certification requirements, reading, learning, figuring it all out. But not much, if any, reflection on the messages I had received. I do not recall any effort to further decode the last dream of me in the pod on that big, big river. No effort to decode anything, really.

My life rolled along. All seemed pretty good. More than one holiday per year, ballroom dancing lessons once a week, latte most days and running five days per week, going to the gym regularly, doing house parties for charity, increasing the number of crocus and other perennials in our flower beds, a red Mustang. All good.

I don't think I would have complained or felt "not quite right," if you had asked me. Life was enjoyable, or so I thought. As I reflect back, though, a soft disquiet had begun. I had started to hear the question in my head, "What are you doing, Joseph? Where are you going?"

I participated in the Coaches Training Institute Leadership program – ten months. That was transformative. Introduced me to myself some. I discovered that there is huge joy for me in facilitating group experiences and that I have a strong intuitive sense in detecting what is needed next to help a roomful of folks make discoveries for themselves. This was not a telling-people-information kind of facilitation. Not at all. This was, and is, facilitation to awaken the inherent curiosity of a person, or group of people, about what they already know about themselves but have not yet accessed. Like awakening the memory learning that I described before.

The "I know" years

One thing that I do recall happening is that I started to slide into the arena of "I know," which inherently puts up barriers to accepting others where they are. Not a landslide, but a once in a while noticing some tendency to slide. I sometimes became lazy and let that slide happen. Fortunately, I did notice myself early enough to take action to correct that, but I see now that it was a symptom of not paying attention to my own journey, of disconnecting from Source, where all answers are all of the time. When I think "I know," I don't bother to check in with Source. The down spiral starts and I drift away from my sweet spot in life, convinced that "I know," so don't need to check in. My sweet spot is unique to me and yours is unique to you. When I am in it, life just feels right, nothing to be tense about, just that nice gentle flow in the middle of the big river on a sunny and perfect day. When in that spot, I was and am, great to be around.

With the ego fear of losses from the many financial disasters from Enron and Nortel and up to the massive financial/stock market debacle in the fall of 2008, I became increasingly depressed. I became angry too, felt it was just not fair. I had worked hard, been generous, had made many others rich, how could this be happening to me, grrrr. We had moved from Nova Scotia to the south Okanagan in 2007, meaning a huge loss in community for me. In Halifax it was rare to walk along a downtown street without meeting someone I knew. I was on committees, headed many of them, contributed in all kinds of ways to the fabric of the community, was featured on the cover of Halifax Magazine and won the Chamber of Commerce Gold Award for Small Business of the Year. People knew me, liked me and sought me out. I was a big deal. (at least in my own mind)

Gone!

I was a complete unknown here. I had to start again to build that network of relationships that I really hadn't realized I valued so much. That sense of belonging to community had sustained me and now it was gone.

Paralyzed again

Was I now paralyzed in a different way?

Indeed I was, I now realize. I didn't know this territory, the territory of living without some notoriety behind me. The population of our town is about 5,000. Most folks here are involved in orchards and vineyards, not much into coaching to grow their businesses or their lives. So, much like the onset of GBS, except ultra-slowly by comparison, I was "falling," losing what I had come to believe was the normal state of the world.

Get an animal into a corner and they can have a personality change, get aggressive. In a way, this, as I now look back on it, was happening to me. Let's change that. It wasn't happening "to me." I was sliding into it, much like the frog in the saucepan of water sitting on the stove and the heat is slowly turned up, because it is not paying attention to what is going on within itself. Before too long we have boiled frog, even though the frog could very easily have just hopped out. I was slowly coming to a boil. I was slowly losing function and becoming paralyzed, at a loss about what to do and failing in the various attempts that I did try. Down spiral. Didn't even know I was in it.

How much of this sounds or feels familiar to you? What parts of your happiness are sitting in a slowly heating saucepan? Look around and don't forget to check the feelings part of you. Where in life is it time to jump out of the saucepan? Questions I needed to ask myself, for sure.

From this place of paralysis, through meditation mostly, I regained more moments of clarity. It became clear that this state I found myself in was my own invention. I had decided that a rural agrarian town of 5,000 was not a place for an executive business coach. And I was cranky about it. Probably a dose of entitlement in there somewhere, even though almost 100% of my coaching is delivered by phone and internet! These two pieces didn't fit. My logical self called me on it. I had an aha from which I began to build my way out again. How? Step one was to notice the disquiet building within (the water in the saucepan was heating up). Then by inviting Guidance in my meditations and dreams. Dreams had spoken to me through my hospital stay, why not again now?

Inviting Guidance

That may sound too vague. So, in detail, here is what I started to do.

1. Confirm that I actually do believe in valid Guidance from "the other side," wherever that is. Without this, forget it. I know this is so from prior experience, but sometimes I forget.

2. Decide who/what I was going to ask for Guidance from. Some folks want to contact past relatives, some like to ask Angels for help, some go directly to their version of God and some just want to access that undercurrent of *knowing* that we refer to as the universal subconscious mind. Not sure? Try this little rhyme:
   a. Fairies, Angels, Spirits all
      Please Guide me, lest I might fall
      Fairies, Angels, Spirits all
      Remind me please, what is my Call
   b. This is about personal purpose or calling but

you get the idea. If a little bit of structure helps, go for it. Why not?

3. Form the highest question, the question that, if answered, would bring me significantly closer to "understanding" what I am invited to do. This need not be all that fancy. In the above example I ask for insight about my Calling. What is working or not working? What is still true or no longer true? What am I really good at, not so good at? What eludes me? Etc. Make a page full of candidate questions if you like. Pick the one that grabs you. Easy.

4. Keep myself in a state of "holding loosely"; allow a range of possible contributions to an answer without insisting on a perfect, 100.00000% "right" answer. This is where the "what if" tool is so valuable. "What if" *that* were a part of a great answer? Remember that the "other side" may not speak my language, but is quite likely to send images and feelings and get me to notice something around me. One more thing – the "other side" can be oblique, indirect, playful even, in offering answers. That means symbol-speak is king. If I notice it at all, write it down. Write it down without judgment about how "good" this information is. Holding loosely is a bit of an art. I practice it and never pretend that I definitely have it right. Just allow it all in. Not working? Laugh.

5. Really pay attention to how I am feeling. The happier I am, the closer I likely am to the good path, an answer that will really help me. If not feeling good, stop and assess my thinking. If I am feeling badly and thinking XYZ, what if XYZ is simply not for me this time? What

would feel happier than thinking about XYZ? Like that. Oh, and there is no "have to" coming from the other side. It is all "invited to," there is never any "have to." I remain at choice.

6. And now ... deliberately relax below the waking state, either go to sleep or enter meditation and bring those questions with me. Some people write the question(s) and put it on the bedside for sleep or hold the paper in their hands for meditation. Some will do this before going to work for the day and put the paper in their purse or pocket. I like to write it on the back of one of my business cards and just drop that into my pocket. All good. Sets intention to find the answer. I often walk around with my hands in my pockets.

I was dabbling with the idea of writing my second book, this one, but I didn't know it would be this exact book. I collected articles that I'd written here and there. I had a misty concept of some kind of book but no commitment. I was paralyzed about what exactly to write. The feeling that I was invited to write it was discernible, just not strong and certainly not acted upon much.

On the work side, I started to make fairly strong appearances in Alberta, especially Edmonton, where I knew my way around, had siblings with whom I could stay, and the population is up there close to one million. A vibrant thriving city in a vibrant thriving economy that was, if anything, overheated in growth and profitability. But I couldn't seem to catch the wave in its full force. Yes things were better, but I didn't feel like I was in my sweet spot again. It didn't feel all that good to keep going to Alberta.

It became inexorably apparent to me that this book, in this present form, was my next task. It felt good (still does) and by the autumn of 2012 I had started in mild earnest. I had written some ten thousand words, but then stalled.

U p to this point all of the historical commentary about the GBS experience in year 2000 have been printed in this font, different from the font used in the emails and different from the font used for the interpretations and reflections about those events and what I now notice, 13 years later. From here on I have kept the font conventions keeping the GBS2 descriptions in this font and the other different font for interpretations and reflections, as it has been. There are no emails included from here to the end of the book.

GBS2

On the morning of January 9, 2013, I experienced difficulty in getting my socks on. I usually go for a bit of a run outdoors before breakfast. I had run the day before, I was planning to go again.

But something was wrong and something about the wrongness was way too familiar, way too scary. I had noticed a touch of "rubbery" feeling in my right thigh and calf the previous day. That too, now, suddenly, felt way too familiar. I had GBS again! (insert expletive here)

I woke Barb, apologized, and asked her, "Please drive me to the hospital because I have GBS again." We both cried. We embraced. We got ready and went to Penticton hospital where I wobbled into the Emergency at just after 8 a.m. The reception nurse looked at me in confusion when I offered, "I think I have GBS." Deer in the headlights was her next communication. She hesitatingly asked me to sit in the waiting area a few feet away. I cautioned her that if I didn't stand when she called me back to the desk, it may be that the GBS had gotten my legs by then. She lost some color and nodded tentatively.

I was being a bit dramatic; it was actually some hours before I could not get up from a sitting position. That was when I was in the washroom and had to pull the "help cord" to get a nurse to lift me off the toilet seat. It was mid-afternoon. By supper, I was bedridden and losing function by the hour. The doctor confirmed my personal diagnosis at around 5:30 and ordered the immunoglobulin (IG) IV (what I called "white lightening") for prompt administration. By 7 p.m. or so, I was in ICU and the IG IV was flowing into me.

Although I was externally somewhat cheerful, helping folks to understand what was happening to me, I was not feeling blessed with my prior too-vivid knowledge. I was in the falling, losing-function state and did not know how far I would fall before the attack on my myelin coating would be over. GBS is a strange thing, in many ways not what people are used to when it comes to disease. Here I was not changing much from an external observer's view (after all, my arms and legs had lost function hours ago). For the next days I continued to lose function. My lung capacity fell to 41% and swallowing a bite of tuna salad sandwich, no matter how long I chewed it, took three swallows and a chaser of water to get down. The anesthesiologist doctor was looking me over very carefully and, it almost seemed, was kind of lurking, ready to move in to intubate me so a machine could do my breathing for me.

I was a passenger with too much knowledge. I knew that I could "fall" a lot further and knew the breathing machine experience was a whole other level of dependency beyond not being able to move my outer body. I was terrified, perspired a lot and cried easily. Thank God I could at least still talk in my vigil with myself. That meant I could ask for what I wanted. Thank you, doctor, for insisting on an ICU bed so that I was watched carefully and never felt left to "fall alone".

Yet, there were some things, many things (thoughts, fears) that I did experience alone. The first dream showed up. I was not drugged, as I had been last time, to get me to stop fighting the intubation. That might yet come, I thought. (insert another expletive here)

DREAM OF THE PURPOSE HOUSE

Day 3. The first dream was of a one-story house, a spread-out little place of a dark turquoise/teal on the bottom half and white on the top half of its single story. It was about 25 feet in front of me. I could see the left end to past the middle but not the whole house. There were flowers, like tall lupines, up to my chest, too thick to see through and an apparent challenge to walk through. Lots of flowers seemingly blocking my way to the house. Lots of teal and lots of white and lots of purple, some pink. I imagined a path off to my right which I thought curved up to the front door. The house was slightly above grade so there was a very low, one-step-up deck, a wooden platform, in front of the whole left side of the house. I could not move, just look. The path was paved with brown smooth stone.

Carmen, our eldest, had flown in to support me and help Barb who was alone at home, waiting. She told me that the house represented my "purpose" and that I was being blocked from fully entering my life purpose. What does one do with information like that? This was one of those indelible dreams. I see it very clearly now as I type this some six weeks later.

Carmen also sensed that I had not quite definitely decided whether to "exit" or to "stay" through this GBS event. I listened to her shared "sense." A big piece of information to absorb. Did I believe it? Was I deciding such a thing? What does one do with such a challenge? I felt alone.

THE FALLING HAD STOPPED

It was Saturday, January 12. When I awoke it was like the deep and almost infinite calm after the big storm feeling. My body had gone quiet. Was the attack against the myelin coating over? I didn't know what to do, what to say, so I just let that idea sit there with me. The next day, Sunday, it was clear, the attack was indeed over, the repairs had actually begun. From mortal fear to elation is a long way to go but I traveled that road in lightning time. I was done with GBS2! From Day 4 onward it was "up."

I am positive that anyone who saw me the day before or for sure someone who saw me on the Friday, would have clearly seen the difference in my demeanor, even though I still could not move a thing. I imagine the twinkle in my eye would have been a total giveaway, but the persons there that day did not have the contrasting images. So I enjoyed my triumphant return alone and then shared it with Carmen and Barb. What a great day!

This knowing place is intoxicatingly WOW. I felt certain and loved and safe and easy, not having to try or perform in any way. That unconditional feeling of certainty was very strong. Knowing with certainty is like having the winning number with all that is left is to show it, don't even have to wait for it to be drawn, just show it. Juicy.

From here the creases in the sheet, the work to even have a bowel movement, all of that stuff, well, it just didn't get any level of concern anymore. I was out of victim into victor so there was no stopping me. Just process now.

I wondered about this feeling and how it came about and more about what it was in me that convinced me that I was the victor, no longer the victim. I suppose I had evidence. The evidence I had was my internal feelings, both physical and mental, that it was indeed over and only time was now needed. The mental part was a "sense," a message from the other side telling me that yes, it is done and I will be fine again. Any other thought would get no traction. Relapse, other disease, something else, nope, nothing was in the way, just time. Ah yes, time, that thing that needs patience to unfold. Sometimes tough for me. How about you?

So touching and helpful to have Carmen take the time and expense to fly in for my support. It felt "big" and grateful and very much appreciated. She has a strong inherent sense connection to that other side knowing place and was generous in sharing what she was "hearing." All bull's-eye information, even the part about not being 100% sure about my staying or going. When was the last time you were given the choice to live or to pass on? See, even having trouble now in using the words "to die." Strong stuff.

Carmen returned home and I had another dream. It was Day 6 of GBS2. The image was of two circles that appeared to be made by, almost, but not quite, drilling through from the other side of some gyproc that was painted yellow, but not very tidy, the paint

I mean. The circles seemed to be about six inches or so, maybe eight inches, in diameter. I could see the center of the circle, as if made by the drill bit of a hole saw like one used to install a deadbolt lock, with the drill bit in the center and the circular saw blade around it. Just there, no movement or noise, just an image but very real.

Deadbolt?

Not sawn all the way through. Coming toward me. Two of them, side by side, but not touching, sort of pointing down at me and about eight feet away in a box/channel between the ceiling and the wall. The untidy paint look was mostly due to a kind of messy white strip on the bottom of the box as if there had been a bit of trim there and that trim had fallen off to expose the white primer against the yellow paint. Looks like heating vent tubes that had not been fully installed, just the holes made ready, but with the tubes installed right up to the other side of that gyproc interface.

Meaning?

I suppose we could make some wild guesses about two lungs, almost needing to be intubated, and at the ready. I didn't know then, and don't know now, but the image is indelible, that much I know. Indelibility has, in the past, meant it is important and I am supposed to get some knowing from it. Sorry, folks. I am not getting this one unless it is that two lungs thing. It could be that the decision to stay or go was the deciding factor about whether the circles were punched out so the air could be pumped in. Maybe, on some level, I decided to stay. OK.

My lung capacity was at bottom, 41%, by this time. And ... this is a stretch, no deadbolt installation will be needed. Whew.

Day 7 provided confirmation that I was on the "up" side of this thing. Lung capacity measured slightly higher, but not enough to convince the respiratory guy to cancel the measurements scheduled for the next day. My voice had shrunk to a strong whisper and swallowing remained a job, yet, with my internal knowing, I felt pretty darn good.

Visitors. As early as Saturday (Day 5) and most days since, I enjoyed visitors. Again, as it was in 2000, some of those who showed up were a surprise to me. I would not have predicted who brought their smiling supportive selves to sit with me a bit, offer encouragement, express dismay and gratitude that I was going to be OK (even though until Day 7 I could not offer much guarantee). The power of positive thinking was what I heard and felt from them. I wonder what their experience actually was. Again, though, I felt the presence of many beyond those who actually did visit. Prayer, I think folks call it. Palpable and encouraging beyond words.

My attitude was soaring as I was firmly convinced that it was but time and willingness to heal that was needed to get me home and back into the world.

Back into the world in a different way. To do what? Great question with an answer delivered into my awareness from the other side. I needed to better understand _and to act on_ the message about "patience and doing something Guided (different)" so strongly delivered in 2000, plus, I was to get on purpose, be my purpose, get to it, act upon my purpose. No more delays or excuses or yah-buts of any kind. Do it! Get into my sweet spot and start now and don't stop. Get over to that path through the tall flowers and walk up to the house. Open the door.

Knowing with certainty

I am amused by how I used to believe that knowing, the kind that comes from Divine, was a rare and privileged thing. This kind of contact with the All, well, not for the masses for sure, and thus the idea that it is only for the few selected ones (i.e., not possible for me). Was not looking upon the face of God sure death?

When I turn on the radio in my car and select a station, voila, there it is. That radio signal is present all around me all of the time, even when the radio is not turned on or tuned to the right station. I believe the Divine radio station is always on and always offering suggestions and encouragement to me. My "radio" is tuned to "my station" only, playing messages for me 24/7, never stops. That I do not keep it on and tuned in all of the time is simply my choice. The station continues to send and resend and does so cheerfully. I am sent what I am most likely to benefit from in terms of suggestions and encouragement toward a happier life. Also, those messages are tailored to what I am able to understand, even if delivered in symbols and such.

The messages are not like on Facebook where if you post at 10 a.m. and I don't open my Facebook until 4 p.m., chances are very high that I won't see your post because it has scrolled down, been upstaged by other, more timely messages. The only One posting on my station is the Divine and all of the messages are exactly for me. The Divine resides within infinity so time is never an issue. Divine patiently offers Its messages. If I don't receive or don't understand It may rephrase but not change the intent/content of the message. My indicator that I have the message and that I understand it, is my feelings. If I feel good and happy and optimistic and so on, chances are great that I got the intended message. If not feeling that way, listen again, open up my antennae to interpret more broadly, play "what if," be gentle with myself and smile. Back to the six steps described before.

Thus, certainty is directly proportional to my feeling of happiness with the message, no matter how vague my understanding. My ego is what demands logical understanding and proof. I just knew that I was finished with GBS2 and I was happy. Done.

This invitation to "patience" was in conflict with the need to pay the mortgage, clean the garage and wax the car, etc. What I have come to understand about this, I think, is that those items are not the list to be more patient with. The patience is invited in application to my satisfaction with myself. I can be very demanding of me. Anyone relate?

That does not mean head for the couch, bring potato chips and find the TV remote. It means release "knowing it all" by myself. Release having to know and having to figure it out without Divine contribution to my understanding. I started to "pray" a lot in the hospital. By that I mean opening to the possibility of Divine connection(s). That meant getting my mind to be as still as my body, to purposely paralyze that relentless thought generator between my ears, so that I could really listen to Guidance. Although I had been meditating for years, this was like teaching myself to meditate for the first time. Slowly and gently lowering the speed and quantity and seriousness, especially the seriousness, of my thoughts became my focus. This is a releasing process, not a harder discipline routine.

I have, over the years, developed a place of sanctuary in my mind. There is a meadow and a sea and a mountain and a "wolf tree," plus a great door and a little ways off, a nondescript building on a small hill. These co-reside in a nature setting and I can see a city with skyscrapers and a Diamond Head kind of mountain by the ocean in the distance. It is completely quiet there. I can invite Guidance here and it comes. Not always crystal clear, but most of the time I get useful direction, even if it is "wait" or even if it is "nothing hot and nothing cold yet," etc. My sanctuary is always inviting and perfectly quiet. I have never met anyone else here.

I am avoiding a detailed description because your sanctuary is going to be yours and mine is definitely mine and they will be different. What yours looks and feels like and what is included will be unique to you. If you decide that you want to meet your Guides and become still to listen and see from within you will find a part of your sanctuary. Your meadow, that place of safety and peace and perfect calm, will look a certain way for you. The location of the meeting place with your Guides may not even be anywhere like this meadow. Mine happens to be. Some people notice the home of their Future Self, a persona used in Coaching. I do not see that. Your sanctuary is yours and you can't imagine it rong.

I believe I am experiencing the same kind of connection that the more famous people with recorded connections experienced. Moses experienced the bush on fire which did not burn and he "received" Commandments for mankind. My experiences are highly unlikely to be recorded alongside of those of Moses but the validity and the value and the wonder of both sets of revelation are the same. As it states in *A Course In Miracles*, there is no order of magnitude in miracles. I say, there is no order of magnitude in Divine Guidance. It is all the very thing that the recipient can benefit most from in that very moment when it is received and recognized and acted upon. Guidance points toward personal purpose. It was the life purpose of Moses to have those experiences. Note that without the acting-on, the Guidance it isn't of much use.

You told me, showed me, how to do something and I did it another way, my own way and it simply did not work. Are we really surprised? So maybe if you tell me again? Please. Maybe then I'll do it the Guided way.

DAY 8, GBS2 (THE CAPRICE DREAM)

My viewpoint is from the front of a body shop that is located under a garage that faces the other way, towards the street or highway. Lots of traffic over there. I and the shop front, face a back street. The basement shop has a rather low ceiling but I can still walk upright. The way out of the shop area is up a narrow, curved (slightly to the right), dirt driveway that is quite steep where it joins the back street, so much so that I wonder if a car would "bottom" as it pulled onto that back street.

The driveway is narrow and there is a '66 light green Chev four-door sedan parked there facing up. Above it is a pickup truck, not quite a '53 Ford, but like that, maybe a Mercury, with a bulbous grill that is cream color. The truck is lovely and is medium brown. The car is not smashed anywhere that I can see but does show surface rust low down, here and there. Seems to be a parts car, but a good one. Another four-door '66 Chev, same color but in better shape, has been driven as if attempting to get up the remaining part of what is left of the already narrow driveway. The driver has

UP FROM PARALYSIS

left it (might be Carmen or Barb or maybe me?). This second car
is extremely close to the one that is parked. I go and find that I
can slide a piece of paper between the two cars but no more. Why
the piece-of-paper image, I don't know. They are that close. No
one seems to be around but me. A shadow or two of people in the
depths of the shop are seen but they are not part of my experience.
I get in the second car and very gently let it roll down (backwards
first, interesting) and steer it clear of the parked Chev. I then drive
it up and simply trust that there is not a car coming from the left as I
clear onto the road. The back of the pickup hangs out onto the road
some, so seeing traffic from the left is basically not possible. Since
I am alone, I just watch for a dust cloud, and seeing none, I boot it
up the drive and pop out on top, swing right and then left across
the street into a flat driveway that I could not see from below, a
driveway for some unknown person's house. The driveway is across
a ditch and not that roomy, but fine for the '66. I then back it out
and down the road to the right and on the left side, the side closest
to the shop. To go further in that direction is a very steep downhill
that does not feel safe. I do this with the greatest of ease.

In the shop is a '68 Caprice, black vinyl top, two-door hardtop with
a deep, clear-coated, brand-new paint job in the same light green as
the two '66 Chevs. The vinyl top has a small chrome crest of some
kind on the side. The vinyl top and the wide tires are shiny black,
though textured. Chrome wheels, not ostentatious but indeed very
nice and the chrome on the car are rich/deep and clean. This car is
as good as it can get, pristine I'd call it, and it is for me. Still no one
around but I know this amazingly beautiful car is for me so hop in
and drive it up onto the back road and, again, into the driveway
across the street. The house is a single-story and light yellow with
some white accents. I gently back out toward the right, careful of
the steep downhill, beside the '66 and drive away to the left. I pass
easily behind the pickup and out from the back road to the paved

main road system. I am careful to go slow so I do not get too much dust on that beauty from the dirt of the back road. All of this feels so natural and easy and, did I say, easy. End.

Interpretation? We owned a light green four-door '66 Chev sedan that drove well and was sound but not even close to pristine. Just a great driver car that the two cars in the dream looked like. I have never owned a pickup truck of any kind, but my Dad did, but not with a grill like this one. Though I have appreciated the lines of the Caprice I never thought it a car to be sought after. Yet, this one was so well done up that one could not help but appreciate it and honor the folks who brought that design into the world and also the body shop folks who did the restoration work. Beautiful indeed. Worthy of praise.

There seemed to be some barriers to getting out of this place, this place that is under and behind. The barriers were gone as soon as I decided to just go for it. I don't recall having any doubts about getting that second '66 away from the one beside it, no doubt about getting up that seemingly tricky driveway or over onto the top road, even though I could not see traffic that might have been up there. I had no doubt the Caprice had been readied for exactly me and that I was to take this beautiful and special car out and into the mainstream of traffic. No doubt.

This feels good to me and it feels like I am somehow ready to get onto the freeway and be proud of what I bring. If you could see my smile right now. The Caprice, like I said, not what I would have chosen, is of note. Is this saying that I don't need to follow the crowd about what is popular and such? A good bit of freedom in that kind of message. A touch scary too, just so ya know.

This may be so.

BECAUSE I DECIDE TO

January 17, Day 9, brought a move out of ICU, a good sign. The doctor was concerned about lack of ability to move, barely able to press the call button, and only if I could get to it. Concern, maybe, about some other things he didn't share with me (so it seemed)? So I was assigned a "sitter," someone to be within voice range to help me with whatever I needed. That included a shave in the morning, feeding me my meals and getting me through the bathroom events. I was placed on a Ward with four of us in the room.

On Day 10 I received three visitors at once, a delegation, if you will, from a group I participate in. They brought food for Barb (Carmen had responded to "what can I do for you" from one of them, who had visited before, with "feed her," pointing at Barb). It was humbling to receive such generous response of care beyond just me in the hospital. Barb needed support for herself too, it was not all just about me. So a few well-made, easy-to-heat-up meals was just the ticket. Bravo and thank you and I cried when they left. In late afternoon I was moved closer to the nurses' station in a room for two.

The patient in the next bed was not quite conscious and would often sort of groan or almost scream (of pain?). The "sitter" asked me how I could sleep in this environment. I thought a moment and said, "I don't think about the sounds, I think about sleep." An interesting response since this other person could be loud and there was nothing regular or rhythmic about the timing. So, loud sounds, randomly showing up, and here I was sleeping. Why? *Because I had decided to think about sleeping.*

That was a revelation to me btw. This, I now recognize, is a great tool. It has some amazing attributes, like it is too simple. By that I mean it is so simple that most people will not believe it can work. Casting my memory back to GBS1 and the pulling off the tape from skin with hair on it and how by changing my thinking, my focus, I was able to override the feeling of hair being torn out. This is that same method. Note here the "most people will not believe it" part. If I don't believe that focusing on sleep will bring sleep, independent of the noise around me, then I would have had some really tough nights. I did believe it. I believed it so completely that I didn't much think about it until asked after the fact. Some people suffer at the sound of a clock or other house sounds so that they are unable to sleep. Hmm?

One can imagine this blocking-out phenomenon by thinking of the flow that athletes experience at absolute peak in their performance. The same happens when I get fully absorbed in a novel or in something at work or a favored creative endeavor. All of these have the common thread of "concentrating" on one thing, which can be amplified to a level where almost all else is blocked from the senses. I just happened, accidentally, or by habit, to use the phenomenon in order to get the healing I needed that is available in sleep state. I wanted the healing with the intensity that an athlete wants the gold medal, so I entered the flow state called sleep. Cool.

Gatekeeper of my mind

The "hit" I am now getting about this is, I am the gatekeeper regarding what I let into my mind. I notice what I am looking for. Going to meet your friend at the mall, you see them and don't see the hundreds of other people there. You see right past or through or somehow just drop the images that don't match whom you seek. It is really easy and everyone does it. So why not apply this focus thing, whatever you want to call it, to getting to sleep in a noisy environment? Why not apply it to writing 2500 words today? Why not use this massive focusing power to find Waldo in that complex picture? Why not apply it to getting whatever it is that you want? Is this magic? Could be. Is it only for others but you and me, us schleps, not for us?

No!

We all have it and we can all use it and there is not a finite amount distributed to us. It is infinitely available to all of us, all of the time.

There is more to this. If I want to find you at the mall, it really helps if I know what you look like. Obvious. This stuff is old news and it is simply not true that it is some kind of lost secret. We all have constant access to all there is. You and me, us ordinary folks have the amazing ability to find Waldo, to find our friend at the mall and to laser-focus our attention to the exclusion of everything else around us. We are "able" beyond our wildest dreams. In the case of Guidance what I need to recognize is a feeling, the feeling that I notice is present when I am getting a hit. When I remember <u>that</u> feeling I have a way to recognize Guidance, just like recalling an image of you when I am looking for you at the mall. Easy.

The only problem is, we don't see it that way. I didn't think anything at all about tuning out the outcries of the person in the next bed. I decided to focus on sleep and sleep is what I got. When the "sitter" expressed surprise, that was the moment I started to become aware that I was doing it. I suppose I had an aha, a hit, or shall we reframe that into, "I uncovered a long-forgotten secret about humankind, an ability installed by Our Creator, so powerful that only a very select few of the people on the earth will even acknowledge that such power exists." Wow, that sounds good enough to get me on TV, don't you think so? Notice, though, that I only started to become aware. In this case of revelation or discovery, or whatever we are going to call it, what I got was a taste, a peek, a hint, but strong enough to get my attention to go investigate. It was in the investigation that more became evident. To keep with the getting on TV idea, more was *revealed*. Is this not fun? This discovery, the fact that we all get to discover, is not new. It has been with us since the dawn of awakening. Something in our evolution has brought more and more of us to the edges where it is OK to seek and it is OK to find. We live in the best of all time... so far.

Day 11, Leslie, our youngest, came in from Toronto and brought me a Starbucks latte. No doubt seeing Leslie was a phenomenal boost but, let us be honest, that first taste of latte was over the moon. She helped Barb a lot with the new and first cell phone she had received for Christmas. I was happy when they visited and vicariously happy when they went back home together. Barb wouldn't have to be alone and all of our girls are both our children and our friends, so a really high level support, all of them. My progress was steady and almost fun. Having experienced GBS before and now that I was beyond any doubt on the "up" path, I was probably the happiest patient in the whole place.

I had "an attitude" about my state. It was just a matter of time (patience) and I'd be back to full function. I knew it with certainty. With the "message" to calm down and be patient so clearly and strongly delivered to me, I started to enjoy the journey a bit more. Function was returning daily and it was not at all long before a "sitter" was no longer assigned to me. On Day 12 I had a "sitter" until 11 p.m. and was then left on my own, which was fine. The doctor was quite careful and attentive about this second-round GBS patient of his. I appreciate the professionalism, the caution, the attention to detail.

Function seemed to be slowly washing down my body. Neck and head first, then shoulder motion. I could fake hand function by moving my shoulders. That was fun, though I did admit the game once I had done my big demo for whomever was visiting. Recovery was sort of predictable. Still a fabulous adventure to "watch" the body come back to life again. Not exactly back to life, but back to responding to my thoughts. The mind does tell the body what to do, if it is listening and if it has the ability to listen. Without myelin coating on the signal lines the muscles are deaf to what the mind wants them to do.

Someone had looked up the GBS1 story on my website, made a copy and put it into my file that is kept just outside the door to the room. Caregivers around the ward were starting to discover it. At first I didn't understand what was going on, but once I figured it out, I would watch a new nurse or physio person come in to see if she had "that look" of a person who had just read the mini-series summary of my thirteen-year-old adventure. A great icebreaker. I took care to learn everyone's name, something I am likely to do, which made relationship-building easier. I'm a relationship kind of guy. Having a conversation with someone who had read the story brought the whole thing to another level. They suddenly knew things about this not at all common disease and they knew things about me. They also had great questions. It was a good thing.

Each day was different from the past as I regained this and that function. I became able to roll onto my side alone and to push/pull myself higher in the bed. Those two movements made sleep familiar again. I could move when I wanted to and could adopt the position that felt most comfortable. I began to do more with respect to eating my meals. It took both hands to push the side of the spoon through the meatloaf in order to cut it, but it got done. As I would say, "not pretty, but done anyway." By Day 17 I had enough wiggle and strength and tenacity to somehow shave myself. I still needed a basin of hot water placed within reach and a facecloth, but I did it, and it felt good.

I recall the jubilation when I passed this milestone in GBS1. This time was not like that. Jubilation? Sure, but more of a recognition of where I was and how the return of basic independence was such a gift. It is like when returning to a most favored place and seeing a familiar sight showing you that you are oh so close to being at your favored destination again. In fact, the first time through GBS I really didn't know how much further, etc., just knew I was over-the-top happy and that I was on the way. This time I also knew how far along the way. A different kind of jubilation this time.

I STOOD FOR 22 SECONDS

Day 17 was also the day that two grandchildren, Annabelle and Zoey, came to visit. An uplift hard to describe. They looked at me, not sure what to think, drew me pictures, told me stories and told me again that they love me. Fortunately, I was recovered to the point where what they saw and experienced was not that scary. Their Mom is our middle daughter, Cathy. She and her husband Patrik drove in with the girls from Vancouver. Day 17 was my first walk. Day 16 I had stood for twenty-two seconds. This day, I walked about fifty feet before almost collapsing in tears of joy. All those walks during GBS1 and how I measured my time to exit by the number of steps I could do in a day and how it all fed me so strongly, all of that memory flooded back, and I overflowed with tears of joy. It was fabulous.

The girls came in on Saturday, drew more pictures and put them up on the wall. Amazing what children's pictures can do to light up a place. Once around the central rooms was the walk of the day, about 225 feet. A new record. My leg muscles were very tight so I really felt them after walking even that short distance. Sunday was double the distance and Monday, well double-double the Sunday round. My body was waking up. What was needed next was to exercise and re-stretch muscles that had been dormant for nearly three weeks.

Late on Day 16, when the doctor did his usual round through, I had asked what his requirements were to sign a release so I could go home. Eat on my own, go to the bathroom on my own, lose the final intravenous tube (a lab measurement had to be up to par) and be able to walk unaided, as approved by physio. Once the goal is clearly described, isn't it just so amazing how we start knocking off this and that part of it, like right away, in no time we have some parts done? I imagined it to be all complete and that it was to be done by Tuesday or Wednesday latest.

Sure enough, I passed the physical assessment from the physio late on Monday afternoon, the last item, and was released on Tuesday, Day 21. Not as big a deal as the release from hospital after GBS1, but plenty big anyway. Somehow I had experienced an event that has a probability of less than one in a million, that of attracting GBS twice. What was next, what was this preparing me for? Yikes.

One quick aside. On Day 18, when the lab measurement was up to snuff, the nurse came to remove that big tape that holds the intravenous apparatus on the back of my hand. I winced at one of the first tugs. She paused and said, "do that thing you did in your GBS1 story so I can take this off and you won't feel it." I was busted. I had known what and how, but still hadn't done what would keep me from wincing. She had read the story and invited me back to that "I am not my body" state. We paused, I nodded, she removed the tapes and it was as if it hadn't happened. Wow, even surprised me. And how cool is that? Big smile for both of us.

So glad she called me on that. It reminded me just how far I had strayed from the knowing given to me in GBS1. How did that happen? I think we all just get complacent and atrophy dulls the memory of the best answers, the best actions, the knowing that is way better than what we used to know. Hmmm, I will call this one of my "take-aways" from GBS2. A good one, I might add.

CONFERENCE DREAM

I had another dream around this time. In the dream, I am a presenter at a Conference with a long rectangular room full of participants. There is an aisle down the center and one across at about half way down this long room. I am walking down the aisle to meet some of the people at the far back, to shake a few hands, do a sound check for my wireless mic and get a feel for the crowd. As I make my way crisscrossing back to the front some of the people suddenly have a white petal cushion, what looks like a low pedestal or giant flower surrounding their feet, about six inches thick. The petals have depth and the outer edges are tinted a beautiful golden yellow. Just a few people here and there and the cushion thing pops up when I pass by on my way back to the stage.

I am wearing a wireless microphone and look quite a bit like Wayne Dyer. It is me for sure, but I look a lot like him. OK, we are similar physically and here I am in this dream about to deliver to a large audience such as I had been a participant in at an I Can Do Conference (where Dyer is often a speaker). If it means that I am to be that person in that room, I'm very happy about that. If it means I am to meet him, well, big OK to that, too.

What does one do after two rounds of GBS? I went looking to understand what I had done to invite this into my life. A dear colleague explained that I had wanted more of what I had learned in the first round. That made some sense if I am correct in interpreting the "be calm, be patient, let the river carry me" message as the theme. At this moment, a few weeks since Day 21, I remain in a state of open listening for Guidance. I ask for it every day and go looking, stay open, for the response.

To my dismay, though, I am finding that life is encroaching on my environment of inspiration and until-now seemingly steady and easy contact with Guidance. I am finding moments of drifting into the familiar noncontact kind of being from before GBS2. Nothing awful, but not nearly as "creamy" as the later days in the hospital and the first weeks after coming home.

Connecting to Guidance

So this tells me to seek the way to get more deeply connected again. What is a method that one can use without the help of being paralyzed? I notice the first sentence in this paragraph says "more deeply connected." I do know that we are all connected to Guidance all of the time. The "deeply" word is about whether or not I am paying attention to that connection. I have the free will to ignore it. I use a structure with coaching clients where I ask them to imagine three chairs facing them (also do it with actual chairs sometimes) and the occupants of those three chairs are their **ego**, their **heart** and their **Soul**. I ask them to describe the traits of each of these persona, these parts of themselves. Which one yearns for peace or love or anything for that matter? Just which one yearns? Which one takes and which one receives? Which one is secure and why? Which one is trying to figure out the right answers to these questions? What does that persona predict will happen if I get a right answer or a wrong answer? Which of these has my best interests in mind? And more questions too, but one more in particular.

Which do I most often listen to?

There it is. That last question is the doorway to being deeply connected or barely connected at all. When you or I interact exclusively on the ego level we get ego type guidance. Connecting at soul level brings a different kind of connection. Soul connection is from a perspective that is grounded in the infinite and all-knowing, the timelessness of Source. When I ask a question from here, I get Soul Guidance, which I recognize as free of any kind of baggage, like doubt or fear or conditions.

The same question posed to the Soul and to the ego returns different answers that are really obviously different. The Soul response is patient and feels like a natural and easy home run all the time. The ego feels like should and have-to and threats if I don't. Not even close to friendly or helpful. Then we have heart, which makes distinctions such as the difference between taking and receiving. Heart does not demand, but will ask and will seek. Heart understands and freely gives gratitude. Heart is open and inviting and wants only good. Ego, well, not so much.

The method, then?

In order to become more deeply connected to Guidance, I need to identify which persona is dominating my thoughts.

I can do that. You can do that. Having identified the speaker, choose toward greater happiness. Use my free will to navigate to hear, understand and use Guidance. From there, life is a beach.

None of this works without intention to find it, to respond to the nudge of intuition. No need to be perfect, as only the ego uses such a test. Heart is gracious and invites another try. Soul understands that every noticing has some knowticing in it and that there are only two kinds of experience. One kind is happy as it is, all by itself. The other kind is a nudge, a learning about what will or will not work so that I can find happier ways to live. There is no wrong or bad, only happy and learning to be happier. Guidance is toward happier, always.

I know, hard to believe sometimes. I had to become paralyzed, twice, before I understood it. And I suspect that I may forget it again as I go along. My plan is to stay in this place of remembering this fundamental bit of wisdom.

Why is this so important?

Some people will read this section first and some at near the end, where it resides within the book. Both are perfect.

The reason I have written this book and the reason that it is important enough to me to do so is that understanding and expanding on the insights I share will, in my opinion, enhance your life. You will be more at ease and happier. People will remark at how fine it is to be around you. Did I mention that you will be happier?

We are an evolving species living on an evolving world. We learn more every second. What was thought to be absolute truth in times past, like the earth is the center of the universe, is laughable now. If you go to the bookstore and peruse the shelves you will find a large selection of books with titles such as *Biology of Belief* (Lipton) and *Virus of the Mind* (Brodie) and *Spiral Dynamics* (Beck, Cowan) and oh-so-many more. These books are doing to our concept of mind and existence what Copernicus did to astronomy.

Other shelves you might visit are all about spirit talk, soul

connection, chakras of the body, energetic healing, angels …
the list goes on and on. These writings are about transcending
fundamentally limiting beliefs about what we are and why
we are here and how we fit into the Grand Fabric of the
Universe. They are also screaming out that we are a part of
Divine and welcomed to be so. No more the message that I
must grovel, unworthy, before a deity that would as soon kill
me as allow me to continue in my wretched existence, let alone
demonstrate love toward me. Some even say that each of us
is Divine, me among them. I say that and I believe that. These
are evolving times and all of us are invited to participate in this
stage of evolution. I want to share what I am noticing as part
of my contribution.

This evolving trend is clearly gaining momentum in our times;
our exciting times. Science is doing what it can to keep up,
confirming the plasticity of the mind against the prior belief that
as we get older, brain cells die off and do not get replaced. No
alternatives? That is old news nowadays.

Most of the present-day concepts have, at one time or another,
been the substance of witchcraft, demons, spirits (the not
nice kind, more like malicious ghosts), generally the occult.
"Occult" has been bad forever. That idea has grown from the
ignorance of the masses, our collective non-understanding and
our collective lack of time to reflect and intuit and learn about
subtle things. Our species has been so focused on hunting
and gathering, which was replaced by climbing the corporate
ladder and keeping up with the Joneses, that the capacity to
access the subtle has not been sufficient to learn much with
any certainty. Plus, if one person learned something and told
the masses who didn't know or have stomach for believing it,
that person was rejected along with their occult knowledge.

Persecution of even now well-known science is common over the centuries. Galileo was jailed for some of his discoveries.

Today is a time of "Maybe there is something to this, uhm, stuff." We have more time to be still and as more people experiment with stillness, more people begin to hear and make sense of what has always been available to us, but at a different level than basic Neanderthal consciousness. Today, it is OK to consider that we are all made up of energy held together by thought. Try that in most of the first millennium.

Snapshot of now

Today, people are seeking. They are interested in learning of the experiences of others and in finding what they can apply for themselves. What I have written about is my own discovery journey. Note that I had a lot of time to be still and to experiment. I was paralyzed, not once, but twice. Though paralyzed, my surroundings felt safe so I didn't have to concentrate on basic survival. I was given the gift of capacity to explore and discover the "subtle." A possible reason for experiencing GBS twice was to give me thirteen years to digest and expand my learning from the first time in 2000 so that I could better absorb and advance the learning that showed up in 2013. Some say we can become expert at something if we read/study for five thousand hours on that one topic. I have had nearly thirteen years to simmer the big wake up calls I received in 2000. I read and studied all through that time.

Truth is, though, I didn't get it, not as I now get it (well, I think I get it). What I now get is that this woo-woo is not only real, it is important, vital even, to future happiness and success as a species. **Actually, it is feeling a bit urgent.** That may be the reason I have felt so driven to write, write, write ever since I returned from the hospital after my twenty-one days with GBS2.

One of the biggest benefits of that experience is that it reminded me of the six steps explained earlier in this book. I started to deliberately use those six steps (see the section Inviting Guidance) multiple times each day. I have become more still, more happy and more certain that I was on the path that was meant for me. I had found my way back. A thousand words a day was easy to write. What to write came to me from the "other side." The important stuff, or what seemed important, I could not forget/erase. An image, an idea, a logic string, etc., showed up in my mind and stayed until I wrote it and then would gently fade. I didn't need to write things down because I had the notebook in my mind, which remained indelible until captured in the computer.

This phenomenon is the "Seek and ye shall find" experience again. Since returning from the hospital on January 29, 2013, I find that this communication with the "other side" is becoming a channel that is opening and staying open for me. It is becoming a common thing to access that other side and to believe it and to understand more of it every time it happens. I am doing those six things and making them into a habit. You can too.

I also "fall off the wagon" often. I need to deliberately make this new way of living, interacting, into habit.

The form of Guidance is not what we might expect. It is rarely a big, arrow-shaped cloud pointing the direction we are to walk. It is more likely to be a moment of slight indigestion or a tiny branch from a tree tapping my cheek or a "what is that?" as I notice a particular color out in front of me. My dreams again became much more vivid, wanting of my attention. My conclusion, at this point, is that the flow of "answers" is constant and rich, eager to show me the way, but I do not access all of the truth available. There is so much. I need to nurture that channel and be patient.

I am free to ask and to see and to then act, or none of these. Free will.

I do not see myself ever releasing or even diminishing my efforts to connect more with the "other side" (though I do blow it often, so I guess it is my wish, not yet my normal way). When we look at what is happening with ever-greater parts of the population, the movement toward Spirit-based living, it is hard to ignore that there is definitely something to it, something good. I note that my happiness level is up. My feeling of safety, in spite of the yak-yak of my inner critic (ego), is strong. I have somehow risen above the basic anxiousness of competition with any number of unknown (made-up) adversaries who were out to hurt me – it's gone (OK, diminished, not gone altogether).

I feel Guided to do things without the debilitating fear of failure that was pretty familiar in days past. A new kind of urgency has showed up. It is not the kind that one might imagine when being chased by a hungry lion. It is different. Exciting, like preparing a fabulous surprise party for someone dear and they are coming toward the door and I haven't lit all the candles yet. Exhilarating without a death-like consequence for not going fast enough. Time is not part of this other view of how things work, not in the same way as we have been experiencing it. Time is elastic now, so it can shrink and expand. Before it could only shrink and add to already high levels of made-up pressure.

Peace and "original sin"

One more observation about how we are evolving is that we are living longer. Some will say that is modern medicine, our greater understanding of germs, disease and so on. (Funny, that. Even with all this greater understanding, it is extremely rare that anyone will give an unqualified black-and-white answer about why GBS happens.) I hereby assert that we are living longer because we are becoming more introspective, more of us meditate and listen to the wisdom of contemplative people. We came through the high-stress last half of the twentieth century and made our retirement fund and then decided to go back and check out some of what was suggested in the '60s. Peace, wasn't that the gist of it? We have more time to check out the subtle. As we slowly peel the onion of subtle, we smile, we remember in our species memory from "the beginning" how it can be and how it may well be just over there, on the "other side." In the lore of the native North Americans this is the time of the 8th Fire, the time to resolve the differences between people and to become "one" again, as it was in the beginning. Interesting how at each turn the message is consistent. Peace.

When I think of peace, the feeling of it, I recognize safety, Acceptance, gentleness, abundance and celebration of differences. As I come to understand, or think I understand, subtle and the "other side," that is where all of those things are. What is not there is the fear-based stuff, the threatening ideas that the ego makes up and feeds, all those distractions away from what I am coming to believe is true about subtle and the "other side."

Another vital piece of this puzzle is that the "other side" is not far away. It is actually inside us. Any separation from it is imagined. In the Bible story of Adam and Eve the idea is that they were banished from eternal happiness, a perfect place, no work or hunger or death, nothing other than peace. My take on it is that there was this thing we call "the dawn of awakening" and in that moment ego was conceived and started its work of separating us from Divine. Adam and Eve were not banished at all, they were just convinced of a lie that caused them to see differently. They "saw" themselves as separated and unworthy and pursued with the intent of punishment. This very idea and the continuing saga of wrong ideas that spew from the ego, this whole thing, is "original sin" from which all suffering flows.

Our species is about to topple original sin.

The Divine is inviting us to do so, has been since the dawn of awakening when we misunderstood and hid ourselves in shame. There are something like a hundred levels of consciousness that we can discern these days. For the most part, even when in deep sleep or under anesthetic, we exist, our human selves that is, exist in about ten of those levels. We are starting to explore other than conscious connection to wherever it is that we exist. I wonder what is beyond ten layers and then twenty layers of consciousness. I am privileged to have been shown some doors held ajar so I could get a glimpse of the "other side." I have a sense that I saw very little of what is over there and also a sense that it is all very, very good. The other fact is that I now have a thousand times more insight about being human than when I started this journey.

I started this journey without knowing I was doing so. Every time I had a moment of "What is this?" that wasn't simply explained by book learning, that was journey material. My child imaginings about making sunlight into energy happened. My request for a "sign" from Above was answered within seconds. My opening to responses from the "other side" has given me answers and Guidance and greater peace.

If I am convinced that I am separated from Divine and believe further that Divine is "after me" to punish me, well, that is a really unhappy state to live in, don't you think? And, here we are, most of us believing most of that. Yuch. Not me. No more. We are here on earth to experience the Divine in the presence of Divine in each other and in the presence of time, emotion and ego (yes, the original sin guy). We cannot be hurt, only die and move on to the next classroom the Divine has waiting for us to experience. It is good.

My motivation in writing about my discoveries is to show you what I learned, why it feels like connection, or better, like re-connection, to Divine. I also want to show you exactly what I did to get to this feeling of deep conviction. I want you to have at least what I have found. I also want you to improve the methods I have been playing with and to then share back. Write your book. Email me. Share so we can all move back into experiencing the Garden as it was meant to be enjoyed. Divine wants us to enjoy experiencing life. Source has given us the gift of this earthly existence and experience. We learn by contrast so some of the time we will not gain top levels of happiness. Some of the time we will. If we learn from those compared experiences our chances of more happiness, more of the time, are greater. Not complicated. Let's get started.

Meditation

They say that twenty minutes of meditation is equivalent to two hours' sleep. That sounds like a fabulous deal to me. Hearing that was one of the reasons that I started to play with meditation. But for many the idea is just not grabbing them. I hear things like, "It's too hard" and "I tried it and it didn't work" and "I don't have time" (Hmmm. Considering the payback in time, what is that excuse about?)

There are misconceptions about what meditation really is. My understanding is that mediation is a deliberate intention to calm the mind, to quiet the yakkety-yak of the ego and to enter a more relaxed energy state. Some say it is like dreaming awake. It is not prayer in the usual sense and is not a religion. Meditation is a valuable method to increase the amount of time that my body has in a day to heal and rejuvenate by releasing my instinctive flight or fight tendencies. Regular meditation can reduce blood pressure and assist with the healing of many conditions.

So why don't people do it? Let me address the idea that it is too hard. Since the typical state of my mind is that it is full of the endless yak of the ego, then the idea of stillness, almost no yak at all, can be too big a stretch, not believable. With that kind of belief, achieving stillness is going to be a struggle. The yak will taunt me and berate me and keep on yakking just to prove the folly of even trying to meditate. Like many things that I don't know how to do or have not done before, I generate barriers to justify my non-action. "I don't have a business plan because I don't have an MBA from Harvard." Right. One of the biggest issues we make up is that we need to nail it perfectly first try. In the case of the business plan, that idea stops many a business and thus they run without a written plan. Way over half of small businesses do not have a written plan. The idea of what constitutes "doing it right" when it comes to meditation can, in some minds, put someone into direct competition with the Dalai Lama. And the Dalai Lama would laugh out loud at that idea – competition to meditate better than another person is just not at all what it is about. So start small, I say. Start with where I am and move toward increasing stillness of mind from here. One is never done, or all the way there, when it comes to meditation. We enter a quieter state of mind, but there is always an even quieter state available.

When I ask you, "On a scale of 0 to 10, where 10 is over-the-top wowzers, how are you feeling right now?" you are able to answer. Everyone can find an answer to that question, whether their opinion of the correctness of their answer is high or low, they get an answer. That opinion thing, we'll get to that in a minute here. When we place the getting of the answer in "time," we can only get the answer in "now." I can't get it from the past or the yet to happen future. My number is from a look at myself "now." So far, so good.

Since, in order to get the number, I came to "now" I shut down the yakky guy, at least for the moment I was getting the number. The yak is where any opinion about the number or how well I did in getting it came from. For the moment in which I found my number my mind was still. I was in meditation. And so were you. It was not hard. What can feel hard is to shut down the opinion that pops up as I return from the stillness. What I recommend for that is to "watch" the yak do what yakky guy does. Let it yak and yak and yak. Your job is to watch. That is all you do. Resist the temptation to engage in what it says. It will try to hook you. Hold firm, watch and just smile at it. It won't be long before our yakky buddy notices that I, that you, are not hooked by what it is saying and it runs out of gas, at least mostly. Ever notice what happens when someone is talking away and the listener turns their attention elsewhere? The speaker runs out of gas and usually goes quiet. Our yakky guy will do the same. When the yak quiets down, even partly, we are meditating.

Longer breath

You may get bored with watching/listening to the increasingly silly attempts of yak to engage you. This is the point where we can fall out of meditation and come back to letting yak prattle along and engaging us in useless conversation within our mind. This is where a meditation "technique" is appropriate. I really like simple. One of the simplest techniques I have come up with is what I refer to as "longer breath." Simply notice your breathing. Don't change it or make it bigger or smaller or anything other than what it is right now. Notice it and count how long it takes to inhale and exhale. This is usually a count of 2 or 3 or 4 on the inhale and the same on the exhale. You have two jobs from this point forward. One is to continue to watch and count the inhale and exhale time. Do nothing else. Let us guess that the inhale and exhale are a count of 3 each. Job two is that, after a time, the inhale or exhale or both will "want" to be at a count of 4 instead of 3, so let that happen. That is job two, to allow the breath to get longer. Back to job one. Notice when another round of job two shows up. Just watch and count and allow.

A few observations about long breath mediation are that yak seems to go quiet when I do this, and, I have often found myself out at a count of 8 and even as high as 12 or more. Using long breath meditation is very easy. No saffron robe or incense needed. I like to do it when waiting, say, for the barber, or for my ride, or while I am a passenger in a car and the conversation has paused. Anytime, anywhere and very effective in relaxing and rejuvenating. One of the very cool things about this technique is that you can't do it wrong. You are just "watching" your breath and allowing it to become longer. That is it. It seems that our lovely brain, reputed to be the most amazing computer on the planet, can barely handle this watching and counting task so there is not the usual room for the yak to do its business. I believe this takes care of any claim that meditation is too hard. Enjoy.

Now the claim, "I tried it and it didn't work." If you were able to find that number inside of you, then it worked. I have never met anyone who could not at least guess at their number. The upgrade to that is to first get your number or guess it or whatever you believe you can do (even if you say you can't, you can do something, whatever that is, bring that) and then to look at your number and whatever amount you are smiling, smile just a teeny bit more. Watch the number. Hold that teeny bit bigger smile. Whatever your body posture is right now, improve your posture just a little tiny bit, and, again, notice what is happening to your number. I have done this with a room full of people and it is easy to feel the mood of the whole place go up. People start to smile very broadly and to even laugh out loud. Many report that their number went up over ten. One lady gleefully announced that she was at 27. The whole room was meditating for the ninety seconds or whatever it took to do it. I am guessing that you were yak-free for many seconds too. That is a sure sign that you were meditating and you did it "right" and that it did in fact work. Go easy with this. Let it happen, or maybe let it happen tomorrow, just don't let the yak convince you that you are not doing it right. Impossible to do it wrong.

The third common objection about not having time to meditate is just beyond my understanding when one considers the equivalent sleep data. I have nothing more to say.

Why connect?

Why is this meditation stuff important? I believe that connecting to the "other side" is the very best path to a happier, more successful life. I further believe that if the yakky ego is allowed to dominate our consciousness that hearing the Spirit whisper Its Guidance is not going to be so easy. I noticed that when I was paralyzed because of GBS and had all that time on my hands, that when I allowed myself to enter meditation, I "heard" the Spirit and recognized it as the Truth speaking to me. I know, with certainty, that when I do hear the Guidance that is all-present, if I just allow myself to hear it, that I receive a little dose of happier and easier and safer and better. I feel better in a way that is hard to explain. I wrote this book to share my conviction that

1. Guidance is available to us all and all of the time

2. Accessing Guidance is voluntary

3. When I hear it, however imperfectly I do that, I feel better in many ways

4. None of this is hard or reserved for an elite few

5. I am to share what I noticed that has worked for me

6. All that worked for me may not work for you

7. Some of what worked for me will definitely work for you; be willing to try... and

8. Some form of meditation is a really simple door to open to receiving Guidance

Why me and why now?

I am just a regular guy, but one who experienced a rare disease and experienced it twice. So I am a participant contributing to an unusual statistic. My life has been wonderful in so many ways but not much in the area of extraordinary. As I sit with this valid question (why me, why now?) what comes to me is, "because the book is coming out of me" – easily, I might add. That is why me and why now. I recall and you may too, back in grade 8 or somewhere around then, that we had to write a 500-word essay or a book report or something like that. That seemed like an impossibly big number of words and I remember writing and writing and stopping often to count the words. It took a very long time and a load of sweat to get up to 500 words. A book is on the order of 50,000 words. Someone who recalls intimidation at 500 words ought not to be a candidate for writing an entire book. My reason remains that the material just seems to flow out. My work on this book has been easy. I sometimes write 2500 words in a day. It just comes. To me, that is valid evidence that I ought to be doing this.

Does this mean I am being Divinely inspired, maybe even Divinely directed to write this? Could be. And what if that is so, what do we make up about such claims? My truth is that many people receive "downloads" of inspiration from "somewhere" and if it isn't Divine, what does that then invent? Every book teaches and shares insight, so why not this one? If I have the feeling to write and can muster the courage to publish, is that not something to notice? Not everyone who feels that they have something to share will share it. Some kind of fear of being ridiculed or accused of heresy or excommunicated or that even worse fate, that no one buys the book. My reaction to all of that has been to notice that I am not getting beat over the head with those fears. I just keep getting the message to write the book. When I am writing the book, things go pretty well. When I divert, especially when I think to "go back to my real job," a kind of tension builds up and the "write the book" billboard shows up again.

One of the reasons for my writing this now, in addition to the timing of the GBS events, is my age. This cannot be a career-damaging move because I'm done with the career-building part of my life. I am in harvest mode and feel so full that I just want to share. A wonderful state to be in, by the way. This allows me to know with certainty that there will be some who will treat the book and me as author with contempt. I have stepped into quite a number of puddles filled with holy water. I also make some claims with only my direct experience and only my own interpretation as their basis. I step out of the line with this book and that feels like my job. That is what I am supposed to do with it. I take the tack that what I have is what I got from who knows where, some of which may or may not have come from Divine Guidance. But it felt like I imagine Divine Guidance would feel, so I'm going with that. I have never felt so compelled to write or so happy after a day of writing. That has got to mean something and I'm interpreting it in my own way. It is an exciting trip with a considerable amount of positive anticipation floating around right now too.

What I have to share with you is as I have stated it. Things seem to work the way I am saying that I see them working. I have those direct experiences and they are strongly etched, at least in this moment, into my mind. They arose with enough consistency that I can explain to you that what I noticed seemed to be the method and sequence and state of mind that brought out the results explained. I admit that some of the experiences are not all that clear. I wrote what I had and did what I could to make things clear. If my words do not make normal sense to you, skip that part, because I don't know a better way to say it. My overall suggestion is that you simply try a few of the things I describe, the few that may resonate with you in some way, even if in an unexplainable way. The rest, toss. Also, as you try some of these things, notice your own variations on all of the steps and the results you get for you. Start a blog or something to share what you are noticing and what you are knowticing. Share.

One of the other reasons for all of this is that I really don't require you to accept any of it. In fact, if you decide to counter and to counter in a big way, great. We'll both learn a bunch. I simply want to do what I feel called to do and to satisfy that billboard image with the word "book" on it. My sense is that the billboard image will evaporate when I am done here. The contents of the book I know to be important but not to exactly whom or why or anything else about it. I expect to be out there on some stage or to be interviewed somewhere about these strange experiences. That expectation is kind of a premonition and I will encourage that set of images into my reality. Since I have expended the effort and invested the time, abandoning my day job in the process, the book needs to be disseminated. Getting the message out there is part of the Guidance I am receiving. I will help with that and follow the echo of that activity.

DAY 60 OF GBS2

THE PHYSICAL ME

To the casual observer I am as I was. My assessment of my physical state is that I am at about seven out of ten. Overall, I feel tired sooner in the day and sleep longer than I used to (about ½ hour more per day). I can trot along, not quite run, and am covering my prior route of 4.5 kilometers at least five days per week. If I attempt a running stride I can only hold a mild version of it for about 200 meters but can repeat that three or four times in the length of the whole run. If I hold the stride short and pump up the cadence I can do that for as long as my fitness level will support and that is growing day by day. When I stretch the stride my calf muscles object. I continue to feel the objection in walking during the rest of the day and really feel it when walking down stairs. My middle back also feels more like a rigid than a malleable part of me. It is like a plate is installed in the middle back. I most notice it when standing for a long time or when getting into or out of, the car. This feels different from the usual back pains I have experienced over my life.

I am not yet able to do a push-up. Touching toes is possible but needs some patience as I stretch down, very slowly. My hands are sore no matter what I do with them. This is something I do not recall with GBS1. Another unique physical item is that some weeks before Christmas my feet felt cold. The soles and toes, in particular, were cold, so cold that I would wear extra thick wool socks and curl my feet under me in an attempt to warm them as I sat to watch a movie. The cold feet and also, later, cold hands stayed with me through the hospital days and only now, 60 days out, are they getting warm again. Still not fully warm, but much better than they were. I don't know what that is about or if it is even related to the GBS, but it has happened. I have been one to walk around the house bare foot. Not now. Another item that I do not recall from the first round is that my toe- and fingernails are really brittle and sharp-edged. Very noticeable. Very different.

I have started to do curls with 20-pound weights and am up to 25 reps. In the recovery from GBS1 I was supported by a fitness specialist who gave me Bill Phillips' book, *Body For Life*. I had access to a gym and did a range of exercises five days a week. That activity took me about forty minutes each time. Now, with GBS2, I don't have access to a gym and just do a few things with the free weights that I own. I am also thirteen years older. The summary report from the physical side of me is that I am mostly fine, though generally stiff and continue to note slowly increasing function. My assessment is that although almost all muscles are "on," myelin coating replaced, that the synchronization of muscles to work seamlessly together is still incomplete. If I want full function, as it was before GBS2, I must exercise my way back to that level of fitness, that level of muscle ability. My ability to do a push-up took around ninety-five days to return after GBS1.

The rest of me

The song Everybody's Changing by the rock band Keane includes these lyrics:

I try to stay awake

And remember my name

But everybody's changing

And I don't feel the same

I am starting to notice that the polish, the intrigue and the almost constant attention on connection to Guidance is fading. There was a book some years ago entitled *After the Ecstasy, the Laundry* by Jack Kornfield. It addresses this re-entry-into-daily-life issue. As I was discovering the many things that I think I now understand, it was a rush extraordinaire. I was hooked by the unfolding and the learning and the fabulous feeling of it all. I felt that I was going "up," if there is a direction to such things. Then a slowing down of the new insights and a steady, "flat" if you will. It felt, at times, as though I had gotten off of a high-speed train in a new land, a land I had never fully experienced before. Today, 60 days after entering the hospital with GBS2, I notice a fading. My thoughts are returning to what I used to think about. My attention is returning to what I paid attention to before. I am losing some of it. Or is it something else?

For one thing, I am noticing the old familiar thoughts and the slipping into the old patterns. That I notice means that I can still choose not to go back, which is my choice today. Good. We love the familiar, feels safe. I need to decide which "familiar" to hold closest to me. The familiar of pre-GBS2 or the new and not too deeply established yet, familiar of the closer connection to Guidance that, if I just think about it for even a moment, is instantly right back here, available, easy, rich and valuable. As the lyric tells us, "... *everybody's changing and I don't feel the same.*" Yes, I don't feel the same, even when I allow the old thoughts to play on me. Shouldn't that be enough to choose what I believe is a better way? The thing that is letting me slide is that I am not paying enough attention, not staying awake to remember my name. When I live in "now," that place where I can watch my thoughts, let the thinker of the thoughts suggest what it will, but keep myself in the place of choice, as Observer, it is easy enough to decide on what works best for me. That best is to consistently discern Guidance and to then follow it. When I don't stay awake and don't remember my name, olde habits slide in unchallenged. Once the older ways get re-established my default thoughts, beliefs, behaviors will drop back to what they were before GBS, whether GBS1 or GBS2, like a comfortable old chair welcoming me back. And is that not the reason I attracted GBS2? Part of the reason was that I let myself slide back into pre-GBS1 thinking.

What is my "name" in this GBS rising from paralysis experience? What is the name I am forgetting, the name I need to remember? My sense is that, in this time, that my name is "seeker." I definitely feel invited to seek and, bonus, I am finding some too. No, I am not losing it all, but just admitting that I am definitely invited, tempted maybe, to let if fade. Nice thing is that I am noticing and naming and choosing to stay connected, but it is a bit of work. The habits from before are still warm. 'Tis all good.

The biggest blocker I have is a struggle to stay present, stay in "now." When I default to running on auto then the ego is driving. And remember it has the low ability and non-courage of a socially underdeveloped five-year-old. And I let it drive the bus. Really? This part of our persona is afflicted with repeated and often severe attacks of seriousness. It gets really bent very easily. I love the song From a Distance by Julie Gold, made famous by Bette Midler, which offers the following lyrics.

From a distance you look like my friend

Even though we are at war

From a distance I just cannot comprehend

What all this fighting is for

Isn't this the summary of it all? My ego mind, the source of all that yak-yak, cannot "see from a distance" and makes up all kinds of fearful futures that are all lies, scary lies (but only if I believe those lies). When I am in "now" I can look around and see what is really going on, allowing me to discard the gloomy ideas of the internal critic. The essential point in the whole thing is to realize which persona is thinking. If the thinker is valid and seeing from "now" and is objective and is not the ego, then my actions will be chosen most wisely. I will know that is the case by noticing the feelings that accompany my decisions. Happy equals yes. Fearful equals no.

Stop. I see something now. I didn't get off that high-speed train and step onto a static platform. I stepped onto a moving sidewalk. You know what it is like when you have been on the freeway for hours going quite fast and then enter a small town that wants you to slow to in-town speeds. I often experience a feeling that I could almost step off of my motorcycle because I feel like I am going so slow. Is that not what is happening here? I have moved to a slower speed of growth, connection, understanding, all of that, and my misperception is that I have stopped. My reaction to that error in perception does not seem to want to celebrate the new, to be satisfied, but to discount the whole thing, throw out the baby with the bath water. Will I shrug and go back to where I was? Isn't that another one of those biggest questions of all time?

Things are different, if I will only pause long enough to notice. I see that I can enter a feeling of Connection pretty much on demand now. Couldn't do that before. Is this not significant enough to keep alive? By golly, that there is any temptation to just let it fade is surprising me. If I have to talk myself into maintaining and continuing to nurture all that I have discovered, well, is it that great or useful, or anything at all? As I try to imagine denying myself the Connection, a resounding "No" shows up in me. I now remember the feelings of safety and calm and ease and happiness that come from staying connected. I now recall how it can feel without a confident awareness of the presence of Guidance, of Source, of whatever we are calling It. Can't recapture those feelings without the objectivity of Observer. Yak-yak takes over and I start to feel vulnerable in so many ways. Do I want happiness? OK, then stay Connected.

How?

Practice, silly. I remember the first few times that I attempted to drive a car with a clutch. Well, lurch and stall and chirping tires and once in a while, roaring off the line. My mind was 110% focused on that clutch. Those first few times were intense. But slowly, eventually, I managed to get the vehicle rolling along and got to the point where a bystander didn't know that I was still oh-so-nervously concentrating on that third foot pedal. It was not too long though before I could release some attention to look at the cars around me, the road conditions, traffic signals and so on. Finally, the task of using the clutch became a subconscious competence. I just do it now. I don't think about it consciously. That means I don't deliberately use the clutch in the same way that I don't deliberately walk. I just do it. How did I get to that state? I practiced and concentrated and I did not give up. I shut down the taunts of the yakky voice because I really wanted to drive a vehicle. It was important to me and valuable in many ways. So I powered through and I did it.

In similar fashion I now find myself wanting to live my life in the constant presence of Guidance. I see myself slipping back to the other way and the benefits of living with Guidance are just too overwhelmingly positive to let that happen. I have decided that I want to do this and I am doing it and it is actually quite easy, now that I have decided. So, to decide is a fundamental part of the "trick." I was once asked by a man who was in the process of a lengthy divorce settlement battle how I had stayed married for over forty years. I only paused for a moment and answered, "I just decided to." The words popped out and may have surprised me as much as the other fellow. This is the same as the deciding-to-sleep incident explained earlier.

So simple? Could that be it? My take on such things is that "deciding" may not be all of the steps to accomplishing things but it certainly is a deal-breaker if I have not decided to embrace something. So I decide, choose, toward my greater happiness.

Remember earlier the decision in the well, to stay, and later, with GBS2, the decision, again, to stay or go. Deciding is powerful stuff.

To aid in my deciding to increase my connection to Guidance and to follow what I find, I am doing the following:

1. I have set my intention to invite and find Guidance and I restate that intent daily

2. I daily ask to notice, recognize, understand and act upon messages of Guidance

3. I believe, absolutely, that messages from Guidance are for my highest good

4. I want, will, feel it in my best interests, to follow the Guidance that I receive

5. I hold all of this loosely, not demanding it be any particular way

6. Following Guidance does not guarantee earthly riches, but it does guarantee earthly happiness. Was Mother Teresa a multi-millionaire? Was she happy?

7. Yes, this is all a choice

8. Yes, this is all subtle and I am making up that it is happening and that it is good with me

Pause to reflect

Will I get GBS3 if I don't follow the Guidance available to me? Heck, I don't know. My belief, at this moment, is that I am on fire with a message for the world. A Divinely inspired message? Well, why not? Regardless, I feel inspired and I feel urgency and I feel certainty and I feel happiness. What is wrong with any part of that? Let the next round of my life begin. I am ready and hot and happy. One big thing about this chapter in my life is that I do not feel anything but fully ready to go. Whatever is needed, I have a great start somewhere in my repertoire of life experiences. Let us begin.

One observation about me is that I seem to live my life in chapters that are about fifteen years long. My first career was in the Navy, fifteen years. Then as a business developer and owner, fifteen years, and most recently as a solo Executive Coach, again, fifteen years. In each of those incarnations I built on what came before and that really worked well. Here we go for the next fifteen years, then.

So I begin. No, I continue, that is more true. That train station platform is moving along at a different level of understanding about life and about Source and about happiness, different than it was before GBS2 and way different from before GBS1. Where I am headed is toward ever greater happiness. I call that the best indicator that I am on purpose, fulfilling my calling, doing what I was meant to do here on earth. I am not a saint nor destined to be one. I am just noticing what makes me happiest and then doing more of that. This is not rocket science by any means. And I want this way of living to remain. Therefore, I pay attention to living in this new way. I also know with absolute certainty that there is infinitely more available to me if I simply go after it. I am doing that too.

No, God will not extend my life. My desire for immortality on earth is zero. There are some ideas out there that long life is a reward and that really wise and holy folks live for a very long time. Those who live long lives choose to do so. God allows it but does not "do" it. How long do I intend to stick around? A great question that I do not have a firm answer for. My experience in the well with GBS1 felt like an option to exit that I declined. GBS2 may have been another opportunity that I, obviously, declined, though if I was offered the option to leave, it was not so blatantly obvious to me.

If, as some contend, we get up to three exit opportunities, then the next one is going to be it. One huge benefit to me from these experiences is my detachment from fear of death. Oh, I am sure that in my last moments I might forget what I am, squirm some and beg not to die, just like some of the characters in the movies, but I don't think so. I have a sense that I am supposed to be up to something bigger than I have been up to so far and that I really do need to get over myself, to go and do that something. I sense that whatever it is, is out beyond my past comfort zone (get over myself) and thus the elaborate GBS taps on the shoulder to help my confidence, convincing me that all will be just fine. I have never felt so open to unknown and so at ease with it, ever.

Guidance attributes

When I receive Guidance, I have the choice to take it or leave it. If I were being directed, that would be a whole different deal. The ego sounds like it is directing me. It is threatening and demanding and yelling at me to hurry up. Guidance feels like the opposite.

A Guide leads, is out in front of me and is inviting me to follow. When I receive direction it comes from behind me, is presented without choice and it seems that I am to go alone. The Guide, on the other hand, says, "come with me, let me show you, I will go with you."

Guidance feels safe, whereas being directed, told without input from me, with urgency thrown in, does not feel safe at all. Feels more like frantic and insecure. It is as if the one directing is not quite sure about what they are directing me to do and that if I even slow down a little bit I might notice the folly of their direction and then decide against them. I am deciding for my greater happiness, based on a feeling that comes from inside me. The voice of the yakker is afraid of not being chosen and thus wants to bully me into compliance for the sake of compliance. It wants to be powerful and to hold that power over me rather than provide power in service of me.

Further, Guidance is patient and loyal. If I do not choose Guidance that is shown to me, there is no punishment, just that gentle whisper of re-invitation. When I am directed to act in a certain way I am badgered, belittled and pushed to agree even though I may not feel ready. When I am Guided, soft whisper and invitation, safe, happy.

One thing that is oh so valuable about my present understanding of how it all works is that there is no competition. There is not a horrible boogey man lurking within the Guidance to undermine all that I desire. No. There is no issue with time since Guidance does not exist in time but rather exists in infinity. It feels different because of, among other things, this difference with regard to time. There is no deadline, and what a great word "deadline" is.

Big gift for me in choosing this path. It is all good.

IF YOU HAVE GBS

L et's start with the good stuff. Although a rare disease, you are not being picked on, unless being associated with the stars is part of it all. Did you know that Andy Griffith, Sheriff of Mayberry, and later in his career, Ben Matlock, had GBS? He had it before he ended his acting career, just to be clear on that point.

GBS is not targeted toward anybody in particular. It is an experience heavy in quiet time. It is a really big smack in the side of the head and, in my opinion, impossible to miss. So, in my opinion, again, if you have or have had GBS, stop, stop … listen. Maybe there is something in this that has been uniquely prepared by the Divine Itself, just for you. Maybe. Have a look. Have a listen. Get still. Maybe.

I have shared my opinion about the personal experiences I have had with the disease of GBS. I feel in a strange relationship with this disease. There was the nurse in GBS1 who almost insisted that I express anger, but I couldn't feel it. I was on the path that GBS facilitated. I was being shown the future and being given answers that made sense and brought a deep peace, even though I was paralyzed and badly off according to the usual measures. From my view then and now, why be angry? I have no thought about the length of my hospital times or the depth of the disease or anything about how awful it all was. I still have limited function well beyond 60 days since the entry to the hospital for GBS2. It will pass. I believe that it will pass. I don't feel picked on but rather more like "picked," as in specially selected. I am happier and feel stronger in every way but physical. But this is my experience and if you have GBS your experience may not be the same.

My suggestion to you is to go exploring within your mind and feelings to see what is there. Notice your thoughts and decide whether or not they are helpful to you. If not, do what you can to change them to thoughts that will be of some help. Experiment. When I suggest that you go "see" I must add that, for me, just because I "look" that does not mean that I actually "see." In order to truly see I need to set intention, narrow my focus, decide what I am looking for, really bear down. One will not find Waldo in that very busy picture without knowing what Waldo looks like, for instance. Nor will I find him if my mind is somewhere else, and so on. I need to decide that I truly want to find. "Seek and ye shall find" is but a platitude unless fully embraced as a life-changing opportunity. *A Course In Miracles* has a great bit of wisdom in Chapter 21:

I am responsible for what I see

I choose the feelings I experience …

And I decide upon the goal I would achieve.

And everything that seems to happen to me,

I ask for, and receive as I have asked.

Thus, according to *A Course in Miracles,* I asked for GBS twice. I prefer to reframe that into, I asked for more conscious access to Divine Guidance. It took the solitude, the undeniable clarity that I could die, the intense sensitivity of my body while paralyzed, all of these and more, in order to get me to notice and ultimately to start to knowtice. This was, remains, my experience. In a strange way my GBS experiences have been a gift to me.

Finally, you can't do it rong (love that spelling). What you find is yours and if in your opinion, you find nothing at all, OK, totally OK. I wrote this book in order to share what I have discovered, not to suggest any kind of measure of your experience. We are not here to play "mine is worse" or "mine is better."

If you have/had GBS, bless you. It would be a privilege to meet you. Thank you.

CONCLUSION

I have offered a number of new perspectives and some new interpretations of some possibly already-known perspectives. Nothing I have offered is absolutely "the right way" to do something or to interact with things in our world. I simply share that what I am finding is working and working well, for me. Some of my offering is tentative for me but "feels" worth exploring. Some parts I have incorporated into my life as truth. I use those routinely.

I invite you to play, to experiment and to learn what works for you, using what I offer or something completely different or even opposite. We each have our way of understanding and doing. Some folks are great with their right hand and some with their left hand. Some are even great with both hands. I remember a boy when I was in junior high school who no matter what hand he caught the baseball with, and he could catch with either hand extremely well, he would sort of spin in the air as he came down from the stretch to do the catch and seamlessly throw the ball with the hand he had caught it in, usually before he hit the ground again. Amazing. So go forth and be amazing too.

Feeling a little bit of doubt or something like that? Great. Go forth anyway. I love the following lines from Lesson 284 of *A Course In Miracles*.

At first to be but said and then repeated many times;
And next to be accepted as but partly
true, with many reservations.
Then, to be considered seriously more and more, and,
Finally,
Accepted as the truth.

This seems to be a common path to adopting a new truth or when the learning is contrary to what we are used to. We need to be willing to try something new.

Thank you.

A Poem by Lin Brian, after her review of an advance copy of *Up From Paralysis*

INSPIRED BY GBS2

And as I live my life, I read
inspiring thoughts, and planting seed
and oft times I need to write
providing insights so that I might

become who I was meant to be
the loving person who is me!
for there is only love and fear
the voices in my head I hear

would keep me trapped, must make them go
replace with loving thoughts. I know
I am the one who has the role
of choosing to expand my soul

with friends... require those who seek
together we often get a peek
of ways of being that spirits lift
as we transform, we see the gift!

Advancing soul... I feel connection
easing path with more reflection
for if I stay so unaware
How can I change the things I dare?

The things I say, the things I do
from a place of love, I want them true
and as I know...
feel this is how
I must stay present, in the now

And ahhhh... 'this better, the way I feel
My life today is much more real
and so more soul-life, for this I strive.
And damn! It's good to be alive!

Lin Brian, April 14, 2013
author of forthcoming poetry book, Out of the Darkness, Into
the Light

No More Secrets

by Malakh Zebulun

The story shared by the author will take you through her journey of child abuse where she experiences a web of encounters by others that go undetected by her large and very loving family. Confronted with bouts of mental anguish; an eating disorder; a suicide attempt; drug abuse and then homelessness by the age of sixteen, she reveals how her learnt experiences and feelings about herself led her to embrace negative and abusive relationships in her adult life.

Many victims and survivors of abuse live in silence with feelings of enormous shame for their plight. The author tells how she hid behind her professional career to silence her own vulnerabilities and shame, until she became desperate enough to reach out for help and begin her journey of self healing.

The author tells her story through her eyes as a child and then as an adult.

She has spent many years working on her own self-worthiness

along with; her confidence, personal gratitude, and learning to release and forgive those who contributed to reinforcing infliction of pain and hurt in her life; whether it was sexually, physically, emotionally, spiritually or mentally. The journey of self-healing was long and hard but she has now broken and overcome the cycles that ultimately devalued her worth; feelings; emotions and expectations for her own future.

The author now believes it is possible to live a renewed, healthy, joyful and happy life when we become in-tuned and embrace our own personal and spiritual purpose and visions for our own lives.

No More Secrets will be available from Amazon

Malakh Zebulun is an international coach, mentor and speaker **www.malakhzebulun.com**